THE GOSPEL IN GORUCKPORE

THE RAJ, THE EURASIANS, THE GOSPEL

HARSHIT GUPTA
DEEP RAJ FREDRICK

Clever Fox® PUBLISHING
Chennai • Bangalore

CLEVER FOX PUBLISHING
Chennai, India

Published by CLEVER FOX PUBLISHING 2026

ISBN: 978-93-7500-495-0

AUTHORS DESCRIPTION

Harshit Gupta

Harshit Gupta was born on 3rd December 2005.

He pursued his primary education at St. Paul's School, Betiahata. Thereafter, he went to St Joseph's School, Khorabar, for his secondary education. He scored 85% in class 10th and is now preparing for the IPMAT examination, 2026.

The first youth to get selected for the Prime Minister's Republic Summit 2024.

Secured 2nd position in the Dhyeya IAS, G.S Competition, and has written a couple of articles for the burning issues in the Hindustan Newspaper.

Deep Raj Fredrick

Deep Raj Fredrick was born on the 6th of August 1972. He pursued his graduation from St. Andrews College. After completion, he got a job in the Christian Medical College, Ludhiana, as a Medical Laboratory Technologist. He worked there for some years and left to join the Northern Railways, Chemical and Metallurgical Analysis Laboratory.

His poems have been published in the Northern Railway Hindi Patrika.

Apart from this, he is a motorbike enthusiast. Covering some of the most difficult routes, Nathu La, Khardung La, and Umling La. He has also set 2 riding records in the "India Book of Records".

Special thanks

To Dr. Göran Janzon and Ms. PC Clifford, without your kind support and assistance, i t would not have been possible!

CONTENTS

FOREWORD

History survives not merely because it is powerful, but because someone chooses to guard it against erasure.

The Gospel in Goruckpore stands as such an act of guardianship. It is a work shaped by patience, integrity, and a profound sense of responsibility towards a history that has too often remained unspoken.

When Harshit Gupta reached out to me unexpectedly to share his vision for this book, I was struck by the seriousness of his purpose and by the quiet determination that underpins this project. Alongside Deep Raj Fredrick, he has undertaken the demanding task of recovering fragments of the past from dispersed archives, missionary records, cemetery registers, and personal testimonies, and transforming them into a narrative that is both accessible and rigorously grounded in fact.

This book does not simply record events. It bears witness. Through its three chapters, The Raj, The Gospel, and The Eurasians, the reader encounters the birth of a community shaped by faith, service, and education, and later tested by political uncertainty and social exclusion.

These pages reveal the lived experiences of a people who built schools, churches, and institutions that educated generations and quietly contributed to the moral and intellectual fabric of India.

What lends this work its lasting value is its intention. It neither romanticises empire nor confines itself to loss and grievance. Instead, it seeks to preserve memory, to restore dignity, and to inform both the community itself and the wider historical reader. The authors have approached their task with humility and discipline, ensuring that the past is presented with accuracy, compassion, and clarity.

The Gospel in Goruckpore is a tribute to a small yet influential community whose legacy in education, faith, and nation-building has been both profound and enduring. I am deeply impressed by the dedication and patience of both authors and proud of Harshit Gupta for initiating a work that honours those who came before him. This book gives voice to a history that deserves remembrance, respect, and continuity.

May it enlighten its readers, strengthen identity, and stand as a lasting testament to truth.

The Anglo Indian Community (poem)

They stood at crossings of land and creed,
With borrowed tongues and native hearts,
Carrying faith in weathered hands,
And learning is stitched into daily life.

They rang the school bell at dawn,
And lit the chapel lamps at dusk,
Teaching children to read the world,
And to walk it with quiet grace.

Neither wholly claimed nor truly lost,
They learned resilience as inheritance,
Building homes where roots were fragile,
Yet hope remained unbroken.

From railway lines to classroom walls,
Their labour shaped a nation's mind,
Unpraised, unseen, but deeply felt,
Like prayer whispered before sleep.

Remember them not in absence,
But in every mind they awakened,
For history lives where gratitude dwells,
And truth is kept by those who remember.

As this book reaches its readers, it carries with it more than a historical record. It carries intent, conscience, and hope. The Gospel in Goruckpore reminds us that history gains meaning when it is approached with sincerity and preserved with care. In documenting the faith, struggles, and contributions of a community that shaped minds and institutions across generations, this work strengthens both memory and identity.

Harshit Gupta and Deep Raj Fredrick have demonstrated remarkable dedication, patience, and scholarly discipline in bringing this project to fruition. Their efforts reflect not only respect for the past, but also a commitment to truth that will serve future readers and researchers alike.

I sincerely hope that this book finds its way into the hands of those who seek understanding, belonging, and historical clarity. May it inspire dialogue, encourage further research, and foster a renewed appreciation for the Anglo Indian and Christian legacy in India.

I wish both authors every success in their literary journey and in all future endeavours. May their work continue to enlighten minds, strengthen communities, and stand as a reminder that when history is honoured, it becomes a source of wisdom rather than loss.

Eleanor Sybil D'Cruz

Author, Educator, and Human Rights Activist

PREFACE

Two years back, during my winter holidays. I was busy completing my vacation assignment. The topic assigned to me for the English subject was to write about the invasion of the Britishers in India. I wrote it with the help of the Internet and completed my assignment. But the question revolving in my mind was where these white people used to live? What culture do they follow here? What food cuisine do they prefer? What language did they use to speak with the Indian people? Some days passed, and Christmas was there, and I thought of visiting a church nearby. On searching for a church on the internet, I found St. John's Church, which was about 10 km from my home. Somehow, I managed to persuade my dad to visit there on the 25th. I still remember the cold foggy day when we were approaching the railway crossing. Nothing was visible

My father was driving the motorbike slowly to avoid any casualties. We reached there at 8 o'clock. But the timing for the prayer meeting was at 9:30. Meanwhile, we were roaming around the premises of the church. All of a sudden, my vision was attracted by a tablet installed near the parking lot, where it was inscribed, "The History of St. John's Church". I started reading and was shocked when I saw the year of establishment. It was inscribed in 1823. On reading the full tablet, I got to know that a missionary named Michael Wilkinson had come from England to establish a church and a village here in Basharatpur. I found it very interesting. Before I could tell this to my father, who was busy talking to my maths teacher about my career, the church bell rang and we all proceeded towards the Church building. We attended the prayer meet, ate the cake, and returned home. I was searching for some more information about the church on Google. The more I searched, the more I was intrigued. But Google was not sufficient to quench my thirst. Next month I will revisit the pastor and ask about the history of the European mission to Basharatpur. The pastor narrated the whole account, and on that day, I decided to research the whole history. I researched for 2 years consistently, but never thought to shape it into a piece of writing. In the same series, I met Mr. Deep Raj, who is a native of Basharatpur and an old history enthusiast. I contacted him to share my views and plan to write a proper thesis on it. I started writing with his assistance. Today, I am here publishing this beautiful piece of research. We both had done a lot of hard work in completing this book. I had never thought in my lifetime that I would do this sort of thing at this age. But it is said, “God’s plan is the best plan”. This has been proved right today. We are presenting this book as a gift to the people of the ‘town of joy’ basharatpur.

INTRODUCTION

When I completed class 10. I was roaming here and there as a Nomad. But the good part of the session holidays was that I got a chance to visit the "Student Corner Library". It's an old reading spot for me. I went there to look for some books apart from the curriculum. I ask the helper to show me some non-fiction books. But the ones he showed didn't intrigue me. I asked him for a book that relates to our city. He had only one book that was 'Shaharnama Gorakhpur' by Dr. Ved Prakash Pandey. I purchased it and came back home. I read the whole book in a week. As I am a 'Modern history' enthusiast, and had also visited the St. John's Church. I always wanted to search for the European society based in our city. In the series, I contacted many people of the Anglo Indian and the Christian community. It was a journey of 2 years from class 10th to 12th, where I researched a lot. I visited cemeteries,took personal interviews, read many archival records, and thought to compile it as a book. It was not an easy task for me. But the person who joined me and backed me through this journey was Mr. Deep Raj.

This book tells about the beginning of the Colonial Era in our city, both politically and religiously. The book starts with the description of the administration and revenue establishment in the district and ends with the chapter of the gospel. This book is mainly focused on the English, Anglo Indian, and the Christian community. Elaborating on the land grants, educational institutions, political movements, European establishments, history of Christian missions, and the genesis of the white community.

Whether it's the English names of the towns like Campierganj, Peppeganj, Birdghat, Bridgemanganj, and Sternpur.

It describes every fact along with a logic. Fascinating Heritage monuments like the Christ Church (1820), St John's Church (1835), Potters Lodge, and the magnificent St. Andrew's Church(1898).

The Gospel chapter advocates the connection of the Christian community with the Europeans. If Christians were inclined towards the Britishers, then they should be considered as the traitors of our country. But Missionaries had nothing to do with the Colonial Rule. On the other hand, the land of Basharatpur was granted by the Governor General Lord William Bentinck. The church missionary society was the Church of England.

Many Christians fought against the British as freedom fighters.

Why did the Christians benefited by the land provided by the mission society?

The book answers all these questions.

Anglo Indian community was more connected to the English because of having partial European blood in them.

But they didn't get any help from the British after independence.

The Anglos still have that trait of keeping themselves aloof from the Indians.

Why is it so?

The Eurasians who lost their white complexion are more friendly?

The Eurasians love their father more than their mother?

If not, then why did they separate themselves from the Indian society?

All these answers are conveyed through this book.

The Christian people with English names are Anglo Indians?

If not, then why did they write so?

Is it in vogue, or were they connected to the English?

What language did the Britishers speak with the Indians during the colonial era?

What food cuisine did they prefer?

What culture did they follow?

What type of accommodations did they lived?

Staying in India was a choice for the Anglos, or were they compelled?

The Indian employees who served in the British government, followed the orders of the government?

So why did these questions arise?

Let's find out by delving into this book!

– Harshit Gupta

The idea in my mind to write and record the stories and facts heard by the senior residents of Basharatpur was not an old one. It was started when I was in my childhood and my parents used to send me to St. John's church every Sunday to attend the Sunday school. Where an old Sunday school teacher named "Dan Teacher ji" told the story about how the St. John's Church and the Christian Community was established. It always echoes in my unconscious and when I became 12 years old I saw the inscribed tablet having the short details of church written by Rev. H. Stern engraved on the wall.

This information again intrigued myself again to search for the history of Christianity in Gorakhpur, but my teenage didn't allowed me to delve into it, but I shared my thoughts to my Grandfather (Younger Brother of my Grandfather) Mr. John Shepherd Fredrick who was at that time working as Assistant Priest (Pastor) of St. John's Church and member of Pastorate committee. He told me about the famous persons of CMS Mission, renowned persons who worked hard to develop the foundation of Christianity.

Time paced fast and I was a grown up now. I was enrolled to St. Andrew's College, Gorakhpur for my Graduation, there I got the access of the Library and I saw the book of memories written by Rev. Wilkinson and

Mr. Bird which re triggered my old dream. I collected the memories of the founders but that time the cost of photocopy was too high and I was just a student from a middle class family.

After completing my education I was posted to Lucknow and was married.

But my dream was not limited to me. One morning Mr Morris Clement (Property Officer –CNI Gorakhpur) called me on mobile and said that "Bhaiya our church want to write the Golden History of our Church to get inscribed on the Stone.

I handed over all the records with proof but looking at these gleaners, My mind re-echoed to the past and made my desire more firm. I restarted collecting the evidences from different sources.. In Lucknow I used to attend the "All St. Garrison Church" where Rev. Henry Johnson was the Priest and a good friend of Rev Roshan Lal (Vice President of CNI Lucknow Diocese and Presbyter-in-charge of St. John's Church).

Rev. Henry was aware about my interest. He desired the same for "All St. Garrison Church, Lucknow". I started again to collect the evidences and records about the establishment of "All St. Garrison Church, Lucknow", which took around 11 months tocomplete and compile and the Tablet was placed inside of "All St. Garrison Church, Lucknow".

One day evening I got an unknown message who asked me about my work on the History of St. John's Church, Basharatpur. My curiosity revoked to know who is he and why He was asking this : He introduced him as "HARSHIT GUPTA" and shared his desire to write an article about the Origin, History, establishment of Christians in Basharatpur.

As he saw all the English Titles of families there during his visit, He was intrigued. The GOD Almighty sent this person to fulfill my oldest desire for writing a book over Basharatpur, I was amazed when Harshit shared his all research and collections about the development of Christianity in Gorakhpur. We met we talked a lot and then we decide to Publish a book not only about Basharatpur but on origin of Christianity in Gorakhpur and nearby.

We worked together and we planned that Harshit Gupta will work on topic of Gorakhpur and I'll work on Basharatpur, on some topics we worked together, after completion It was upon Harshit to contact the suitable Publisher for publishing the book and I'll bear the finance.

And now the labor of continuous research, compilation, collection, Interviews, personal meetings, visiting different places : The Gospel in Goruckpore comes out from a dream to reality.

For all this I thank to "My GOD ALMIGHTY and My Lord YESHUA (Jesus Christ)" for giving me "Harshit Gupta" as a messenger to complete my Oldest dream in reality.

I also want to thank my dear friend Mr. Morris Clement (Director of Lucknow Diocesan Trust Association (LDTA) and Property Officer of Gorakhpur Deanery,CNI) for his unconditional help and support.

– Deep Raj Fredrick

THE RAJ

Administration and Revenue

Gorakhpur was, in the early days, the headquarters of a division which included the modern districts of Gorakhpur, Basti, Azamgarh, and part of Ballia; but after the Mutiny, the whole was merged in the Benares division, the present commissionership of Gorakhpur, comprising this district, Basti, and Azamgarh, dating from the 1st of April 1891. The district is in charge of a magistrate and collector, whose sanctioned staff consists of two covenant assistants with full powers, six deputy collectors with full powers, and one gazetted officer with less than full powers, in addition to six tahsildars.

Till within comparatively recent times, Gorakhpur was a cantonment for native troops, accommodating a regiment of infantry, and before the Mutiny, artillery and cavalry also were quartered there. The cantonment has been abolished, and in 1904 it was given up by the military authorities, although the place still serves during the cold weather as a recruiting depôt for Gurkhas.

Apart from this, the only military force is a squadron of the United Provinces Horse and the Bengal and North-Western Railway Volunteer Rifles, both with headquarters at Gorakhpur

The fiscal history of the district begins with the cession of Gorakhpur to the Company in November 1801.Mr. Routledge, the first collector, appointed tahsildars for the purpose on a fixed salary, together with a percentage of the collections, should these amount to a reasonable proportion of the nominal demand.

Forest Grants

Mr. Bird, with a view to bringing under cultivation the large tracts of waste land and jungle. In most cases, the land was granted for fifty years on what were considered to be particularly favourable forms, subject to a progressive demand,

The experiment was attended with marked success, and very large grants were made to several well-to-do Europeans. The first grant was that of Basharatpur, 1,120 acres in extent, given to Mr. Wilkinson in 1880, and in the next ten years no less than 618,547 neves were distributed in this manner, 418,000 acres being in the hands of Europeans. Much of this lay in Basti, and in the present Gorakhpur district, there were 22 grants with an area of $10,220 acres. The largest were the Lehra and

Bargaona grants in the Haveli and Binayakpur parganas, with an area of 69.920 acres, given to Mr. Bridgman; the three grants of Sonari, in pargana Tilpur, Bhainsaha in Sidhua Jobna and Sumbhakhor in Haveli, aggregating 63,148 aeres, given to Mr. Finch; the tlirce grants of Bargaon Chaura in Sidhua Jobna, and Bhilaunt and Bhilampur in Havoli, 55,780 acres in all, held by Mr. Sym; the Banki, Rasulpur and Keotali grants of 35,372 aeres in Haveli held by Mr. Fitzgerald; the two grants of Majhar and Lehra, 82,169 acres in all, given to Mr. Debnam; and Lady Malkin's grant of Nagwa, comprising 23,200 acres in

Binayakpur. Others of considerable size were Mr. Campier's two grants of Bhari Bajay and Kauria in Haveli, covering 17,624 acres; the two grants of Bhawar in Tilpur with an area of 18,048 acres, given to Mr. Downes, and the Ramgarh grant of 11,198 acres in Haveli held by Mr. MoCornish. Besides these, there were three small grants comprising Belwar in Haveli, 4,714 acres, owned by Mr. Morais, Kahistan in Tilpur, 1,932 acres, held by Mr. Hastings and Mr. Wilkinson's grant of Basharatpur already mentioned.

Hence it has happened that, while six of the seven grants held in the latter district by Europeans in 1846 are still flourishing, only four of the 22 in Gorakhpur have survived. The Sonari grant is now reserved forest;

Ramgarh and Rasulpur were sold to various zamindars; Barguon Chaura, also known as Jangal Padrauna, was bought intact on Mr. Sym's death by Rai Madan Gopal Rai, and now forms one of the most valuable parts of the estate held by his descendant, the present Raja of Padrauna; Mr. Tucker had conducted an investigation in 1846 into the conditions of the grants with the result that 280,179 acres, mainly in this district, were resumed and retained by Government as reserved forest or made over to the original settlers. In 1872, the existing grants covered an area of 362,035 acres, of which 194,414 were under cultivation.Hence, it has happened that, while six of the seven grants held in the latter district by Europeans in 1846 are still flourishing concerns, only four of the 22 in Gorakhpur have survived. The Sonari grant is now a reserved forest; Ramgarh and Rasulpur were sold to various zamindars; Bargaon Chaura, also known as Jangal Padrauna, was bought intact on Mr. Sym's death by Rai Madan Gopal Rai, and now forms one of the most valuable parts of the estate held by his descendant, the present Raja of Padrauna;Of the estates which have survived, the largest and by far the most important is that of Lehra, situated in the Lehra tappa of pargana Haveli in the Maharajganj tahsil. It was granted originally in 1883 to Mr. J. H. Bridgman and then consisted of 50,800 acres of forest and grass plains. By 1840 BOTO 12,500 acres of the grass lands and 6,500 acres of forest had been cleared and brought under cultivation at great expense, when the outbreak of an epidemic caused the death or the dispersal of the tenants, Even to-day the sawyers who work for the railway sleeper con-tractors in the forests of Nepal invariably commence operations by doing puja to the guardian spirits; and Mr. Bridgman tells of the desertion of a large body of labourers because one or two of their number were tripped up by concealed stumps when ploughing. Despite every effort, it was found impossible to obtain tenders at remunerative rents, and in 1848, Mr. Bridgman resigned 25,000 acres of his grant.Mr. Bridgman died in 1892, and the estate passed to his former manager and son-in-law, Mr. J. J. Holdsworth, C. I. E., the present owner, on whose behalf it is managed, during his absence, by Mr. F. Howard. South of Lehra, on the borders of the Sadr tahsil, lies Bhilaunji, representing part of the Bhilaunji and Bhilampur grants made originally to Mr. Sym. This property was split up and sold, some 1,700 acres, known as Agahi and Bahli, being bought by the Babus of Tighra. The lands of the latter were confiscated for rebellion, and the two plots, together with eleven jogir villages, were given to Mr. William Peppe in recognition of services rendered by him during the Mutiny. The Bhilaunji estate thus passed on the death of Mr. Peppe to his heirs, Messrs. W. C. and G. T. G. Peppe and their sister Mrs. Larpent, who are also part owners of Birdpur and Alidapur in Basti. Mr Peppe used to play golf in Peppeganj. They reside in England, and the whole property is managed on their behalf by Mr. D. Ricketts. On this estate, there are considerable protective works on the banks of the Rohin, consisting of a bandh more than three miles in length with masonry sluice-gates, and a second bandh over two miles long, which protects the lowlands in the vicinity of the Rapti. The Bhari Baisi grant between Lehra and Bhilaunji and the Kauria grant to the south of Bhilaunji were originally given to Mr. J. Campier.

He left three sons, Messrs. J. C. Campier, E. Campier, and A. Campier; but the second sold his share to the first, and the third died without issue, so that the whole estate will once more be concentrated in the possession of a single party, Mr. A. Campier's widow having only a life interest in his share of the property. Mr. J. C. Campier died some years ago, leaving a daughter and a widow, of whom the former was subsequently married to Mr. Argles, now deceased, and her children are the heirs to the whole estate. It should be mentioned that Kauria belongs entirely to Mrs. Argles, and only Bhari-Baisi was divided between the three brothers. The former is 7.352 acres in extent and pays a revenue of Rs. 7,720, while the latter covers 2,776 acres assessed at Rs. 2,154.

Mr. Wilkinson, the recipient of the first grant made to a European, was the C. M. S. missionary stationed at Gorakhpur, as already mentioned on a previous page. The grant, known as Jurgal Wilkinson, was 1,128 acres in extent and was brought under cultivation by converts attached to the mission. A village sprang up on the spot and was appropriately named Basharatpur: it is still a flourishing Christian settlement, possessing a church and a school, and is under the care and superintendence of the representative of the C. M. S. at Gorakhpur. The present area is 967 acres, and the revenue demand is Rs. 990.The privilege is said to have been granted originally by the Raja of Satasi and has always been recognised by the British Government.

Indigo Concern

In the early years of the last century, the cultivation of Indigo. indigo seems to have been quite unimportant, and it was not till 1838 that the crop attracted much attention. The settlement report of that year refers to its successful introduction in the forest grant of Mr. Sym and its cultivation at Babhnauli in pargana Sidhua Jobna. From that time forward, the area under indigo showed a rapid and constant increase, and by the time of the seventh settlement amounted to 33,000 acres, despite the setback caused by the Mutiny. Nevertheless, the crop oven at that time was unpopular with the cultivators, who showed a decided preference for sugarcane and opium, and towards the end of the settlement, the area showed a marked decrease, the total in 1888 being only 18,907 acres.The bulk of the indigo is cultivated on behalf of the Babhnauli factory, which is now the only concern of importance. The dye is manufactured both at Babhnauli and at three outworks located at Domath, Baikunthpur, and Sapaha.This place is well-known as the headquarters of a large factory, now managed and partly owned by Mr. F. Mackinnon. Babhnauli is one of the oldest indigo factories in the district, and is still the centre of the industry; the proprietor has a fine residence here, while the factory is well furnished with the various apparatus employed in the preparation of the dye.

With so variable a product as indigo, it would be misleading to give the average outturn of the dye for a term of years, but it may be stated that in a good season, the amount of indigo manufactured varies from 2,000 to 2,500 maunds, the whole of which is exported to Calcutta. The decline in cultivation is, of course, due to the competition from the synthetic dye.

Of late years. However, the extent of this form of irrigation has been much reduced, owing to objections raised by the Nepalese authorities to the building of the dams, while the supply of water has diminished with the construction of similar embankments by the cultivators in Nepal. Of more importance is the canal system on the Lehra estate, now held by Mr. J. J. Holdsworth.

Whatever trade the district may have possessed in former days seems to have disappeared wholly under the malign influence of Oudh rule. In 1802, the collector, Mr. Routledge, reported that the amil had wrung the last remnant of wealth from the desolated province, that despite the fertile soil, nothing was grown beyond the bare necessaries of life, and that the produce was barely sufficient for local consumption. Nevertheless, the officers of the Company were so jealous of the trade monopoly that from the first they endeavoured to restrain private enterprise, and they actually expelled from the district a Mr. McCleish who asked permission to build a bungalow.

In 1806 another application made by a Mr. Yeld to build a bungalow and cultivate indigo, though strongly supported by the collector, was vetoed by the Governor-General; and it was not till 1830 or thereabouts that this policy was abandoned, since as late as 1827 the Supreme Government expressed fears that English and other European interlopers, "often men who have accumulated money by embezzlement," were attempting to take the whole trade of the country into their hands. By 1816, a considerable traffic in cloth, sugar, and saltpetre had grown up with Benares, and in 1820 it appears that an ad valorem duty of 5 per cent., a precursor of the modern octroi, was levied on all goods coming into Gorakhpur

Buchanan was able to state that by 1815 or thereabouts, most commodities were transported by road, while in 1830, Mr. Reade, with fine optimism, declared the routes to Nepal, Oudh, Saran, Ghazipur, and Tirhut to be in excellent order. The necessity for qualifying this statement is proved not only by the complaint of a writer in 1837 that some of the roads seemed to have been constructed "merely for the convenience of gentlemen going on shooting parties," but also by the fact that communications for long remained in a deplorably backward state. The Campiers of campierganj also had a considerable indigo cultivation.

Jail

Soon after 1610, Raja Basant Singh attacked and expelled the Muhammadan garrison and built a fort on the site of the old jail in the Basantpur muhalla.There appears to have been a jail at Gorakhpur from the earliest days of British rule, but the site of the first building is no longer traceable. Between 1840 and 1845, a second jail was erected in Muhalla Basantpur, on the site of Raja Basant Singh's fort, overlooking the Rapti. This building proved very unsatisfactory, and the health of the prisoners suffered to such an extent that in 1889 an enquiry was made, with the result that the jail was condemned. Accordingly, a new first-class jail, the most modern of its kind in the United Provinces, was built in 1894-95 to the south-east of the road to Pipraich and to the north of the railway settlement. The old buildings were demolished, save for a portion made over to the Opium department in 1903. The new jail is an extensive brick structure, covering an area of 19 acres; it has been in use since the beginning of 1897, and is under the superintendence of the civil surgeon.

Irrigation

The embankment began by Mr. Tucker when collector in 1845 and was completed five years later. A dam was erected known as Tucker Bandh

Education

There were 243 Persian, 170 Sanskrit, and 15 Hindi schools in this district and Basti, with an aggregate of 3,508 scholars, and the collector remarked that the whole of the vast population was in a state of utter ignorance save for some Brahman astrologers, several Kayasth officials, and a few respectable Muslims. A free school had been started at Gorakhpur in 1835, under the management of a local committee, but it failed to succeed and was broken up after an existence of nine years. The Church Missionary Society's school was started in 1844, and for a long time was the only educational institution of any importance in the district. Village schools on the halqabandi system were first opened in May 1856, and at the same time, tahsil schools were established at Salempur, Pipraich, and Sahibganj; but the work thus begun was interrupted by the Mutiny, and when the schools reopened in 1858, there were but 52 pupils in the tahsil and 108 in the eleven village schools. In addition, there was the C. M. S. school with 180 scholars and 96 indigenous schools with an attendance of 793. Ten years later, in 1868, the numbers were much larger. Besides the C. M. S. high school and the orphanage, there were 176 halqabandi schools with 9,505 scholars, 11 girls' schools with 281 on the rolls, 185 indigenous schools with 2,243 pupils, and 14 middle schools with an attendance of 1,116.

Several of the more important schools are maintained by the C. M. S., including St. Andrew's College, teaching up to the first arts standard, a high school, an anglo-vernacular school, a vernacular middle school, and five primary schools for boys, the number of pupils being 935 in all. The history of the mission and its development has been given elsewhere. The Jubilee High School was built originally as an oriental zila school in 1875, and was reconstituted in 1887 as a municipal high school. In 1907, it was handed over to the district board, and it is now intended to convert this most flourishing and popular institution into a provincial school under the immediate control of the Department of Public Instruction.

A school of the catholic diocese, "St. Mary School," was added in 1941. A new inter College King Edward (1912) was later established in Deoria by J Hope Simpson Esq. Another was the King George School (1924) in Barhaj laid by Mr. A.C Holmes Esq.

Dispensary

The Dufferin hospital has accommodation for 22 patients, and is supported partly by contributions from the municipal and district boards, partly by subscriptions, and partly by the income from a small endowment, the whole amounting to Rs. 1,450 per annum a railway dispensary for the servants of the Bengal and North-Western Railway Company.

A dispensary and Hospital was erected in Padrauna by the Raja and are named Victoria Memorial Hospital.

Animal

The proximity of Nepal and the wide extent of forest are responsible for the presence of an unusually large number of wild animals and a considerable diversity of species. There has, however, been a great reduction in the case of the larger animals during the past fifty years, and Gorakhpur no longer presents the same attractions to the sportsmen which it offered in early days. It is related that in 1856, the mails to Padrauna were stopped by the tigers, which then infested the roads, and as late as 1873, a tiger was shot by the magistrate in Gorakhpur itself.

The wild buffalo has disappeared, the last specimen having been obtained in 1896, and the rhinoceros has long ceased to be a resident of this district, though isolated instances are on record of such animals being carried down the Gandak from Nepal by floods. Of the larger carnivora, the leopard is still fairly common, but the wolf is almost unknown. Bears are occasionally seen, and the wild pig is common, especially in the lowlands of the Ghagra. Several varieties of deer inhabit the forests, but the chital or spotted deer alone occurs in any numbers. Antelopes are somewhat abundant in the shape of the black-buck and the nilgai, the latter resorting to the jungles and also to the Ghagra diwara lands. Other animals include jackals, foxes, hares, porcupines, and monkeys, while in the rivers the alligator, gorilla, and porpoise are frequently to be seen. Snakes are common, especially the cobra and krait, which are most often seen during the rains, and the python is occasionally found in the north.

Christianity

The number of Christians at the last census was 1,443, and of these, 1,040 were natives, the latter figure having risen from 808 in 1881 and from 852 ten years later. Of the native Christian community, 731 belonged to the Anglican communion, which also probably included some of the 300 persons in whose case no specific denomination was returned. The Gorakhpur Mission was founded by Mr. R. M. Bird, who in 1821 raised a sum of money from the residents of the station and applied to the Church Missionary Society for a missionary chaplain. Three years later, the Rev. Michael Wilkinson arrived to take up the work at Gorakhpur, and in 1831, he obtained from Lord William Bentinck the grant of 2,000 bighas of unreclaimed forest to be brought under cultivation by the converts, and on this property stands the Christian village of Basharatpur. In 1854, the Rev. H. Stern came to the Gorakhpur mission, and during the forty years of his incumbency, the work was greatly extended. The village of Sternpur was established in 1881, and the hamlet of Dharampur was added in 1884. The inhabitants of these villages are principally cultivators, but some are employed on the railway as guards, signallers and clerks. Much attention is paid to industrial training, and the women and girls are particularly expert in drawn-thread work, which commands a ready sale, while the boys are employed in the carpenters' shop and the Church Missionary Society Press, which does a good deal of job-work in the city. The educational work of the mission is of great importance, but is non-denominational. The chief institution is St. Andrew's College, which was raised to its present status in 1899.

Attached to it is a high school, and in addition, there is an Anglo-Vernacular middle school in Alinagar, the Swinton Memorial Vernacular Middle School in Sahibganj, and five primary schools. In connection with the Church Missionary Society is a branch of the Zanana Bible and Medical Mission, which has two ladies, Miss Booth and Miss Powell, working in the city and managing primary schools for girls. Evangelistic work is carried on during the cold weather in the district, but nowadays conversions are not common, and the numbers of the Christian community are increased mainly by the natural growth of the three villages and by the agency of the orphanages. There are two churches at Gorakhpur. Christ Church, the old station church, was built in 1829 by private subscription, and St. Andrew's owes its origin to the railway company, by which was built in 1898. The senior Church Missionary Society missionary acts as chaplain to the station.

Literature

The first of these, the Riaz-ul-Akhbar, an Urdu publication appearing every fourth day, was started in 1881, but in 1907 was moved to Lucknow. The editor, Hakim Barham, started a newspaper called the Mashriq a month later, this being an Urdu weekly with a circulation of some 600 copies devoted to local news and correspondence on social, religious, and political matters. The same person owns a weekly conno paper, also in Urdu, entitled the Itr-i-Fitna, which contains contributions in verse and prose as well as illustrations; it was suspended in 1898, but was resuscitated in 1903. There are at present eight printing presses in the district, all at Gorakhpur excepting the Masudi press at Bharauli in the Deoria tahsil. The most important belongs to the Church Missionary Society, and contains a large Wharfedale printing machine and one press; it undertakes all kinds of printing in English and lithography. The Dinapur press is a hand press doing miscellaneous job work in English.

A purely social open-air club, called the Union Club, meets in the grounds of the Masonic Lodge, and books and newspapers are provided for the members, who for the most part belong to the legal profession.

Telegraph

The lines of telegraph are carried along the railway, except that from Gorakhpur to Kasia, and its extensions to Padrauna and Tamkuhi, at each of which places are combined post and telegraph offices. The latter exists also at Deoria, Majhauli aud Barhaj, while there are railway offices at the various stations on the main line and its several branches.

Inspection Bungalow

Inspection Bungalows are present in Bansgaon, Sahjanwa, and Deoria

War with Nepal

This was based on Gorakhpur and was commanded by General J. S. Wood, who was ordered to march through Butwal into Palpa, his force comprising 14 guns and some 4,000 infantry, including the 17th Foot. The story of his exploits is not inspiring. He reached Batwal without opposition on the 3rd of January 1815, to find the pass in which the town is fortified and held by a force under Wazir Singh.

In the meanwhile, Ochterlony had conquered Dehra Dun and Kumaun, but the Gurkhas were unwilling to accede to the terms demanded and to relinquish the Tarai; so that preparations were made for a second campaign, and Colonel Nicholls was placed in command at Gorakhpur for the advance on Butwal and Palpa. The negotiations, however, lingered on till the end of October, with the result that a compromise was reached and a treaty was signed at Sigauli on the 28th of November. It soon transpired that this step was merely intended to deceive; for the treaty was never ratified, and in February 1816 it became clear that the Nepalese intended to continue the war. On this occasion, Sir David Ochterlony entered Nepal from Bihar, completing the campaign by the beginning of March. The treaty was then accepted, and all the Tarai between the Sarjn and the Gandak, excepting Butwal proper, was given up to the British.

Gurkha Recruitment Depot

Lt. Gen William Birdwood

1. Gorkha Recruiting Depot (GRD), Kunraghat, is located in Gorakhpur. The present location was chosen due to its proximity to the Indo-Nepal Border and also being the nodal point of all roads leading to the hilly districts of Central and Western Nepal. Gorakhpur is conveniently located on the main NER Broad Gauge Lucknow-Assam line.
2. Gorkha Recruiting Depot (GRD), Kunraghat, is the oldest establishment of its kind in the Indian Army. This station came into being as the Gorkha Recruiting Depot (GRD) in the year 1886. The prime task of

Gorkha Recruiting Depot, Kunraghat, is to conduct recruitment of Nepal-domiciled Gorkhas (NDGs) from the Central & Western Nepal into the Indian Army. Based on the experience gained from Gorkha Recruiting Depot (GRD), Kunraghat, the Britishers expanded their recruitment drive to other Regiments and regions in India. In 1890, the Gorkha Recruiting Depot was also established at Ghoom (Darjeeling) for the recruitment of Nepalese Gorkhas from Eastern Nepal, and also for the recruitment of Indian Gorkhas from the Darjeeling District of West Bengal

3. Before this, the British had five Gorkha Regiments of a battalion each. However, there was no formal recruitment for Gorkhas from Nepal. As no treaty existed with Nepal on the subject of recruitment of Nepalese into the British Regiments, the latter enrolled NDGs by sending recruiting teams into the hills to bring potential recruits to the Regiment Headquarters. When Maharaja Bir Shamsher became the King of Nepal in 1886, the relations between the British in India and the Nepalese authorities improved. Consequently, the Nepalese regime permitted the recruitment of Gorkhas into the British Army from their country. During the First World War, over two lakh Gorkhas were enrolled into the British Army.
4. This Depot is now spread over an area of 104 acres and has grown from strength to strength over the

years. Gorkha soldiers are proud of its rich heritage and rightfully consider this Recruiting Depot as their "Mecca", since it has served their cause for generations.

According to records, William Birdwood was the commander-in-chief in the year 1917

Raja of Gopalpur

Up to the Mutiny, the Raja was the owner of Barhalganj, but on the confiscation of his property, the place was taken under direct management. Some of the land was bestowed on the loyal Raja of Gopalpur, but the latter was soon obliged to sell it in order to pay his debts, and the present owners are the Mahant of Paikauli and Maulvi Subhanullah of Gorakhpur.

Next reward was a grant from the village of Dhuriapar Bridgmanganj

Bridgmanganj, formerly known as Sahibganj, is named after Mr. J. H. Bridgman, the first grantee of the Lehra estate, and lies in 27° 11′ N. and 83° 12′ E., at a distance of nearly 40 miles north-west from Gorakhpur, and three miles west of Mr. Holdsworth's house at Lehra. It is connected with the roads from Gorakhpur to Uska and Lotan, while close to the bazar on the south is a station on the railway to Uska and Tulsipur. The construction of the line has attracted much of the trade with Nepal, which formerly accumulated at Dhani, some six miles to the south. The place is now a thriving market, and the bazaar contains a good number of brick-built houses. The population numbered 1,727 persons in 1901 and has since increased to a considerable extent. Bridgmanganj contains a branch post office, Tower primary school, and an aided Sanskrit pathshala, while at Bela Haraayas, about a mile to the west, is a dispensary maintained by the district board. The residence of Mr. Holdsworth, known as Park House, stands about a mile and a half north-west along a metalled road from the Lehra station on the railway. The house is a handsome and spacious building standing in extensive grounds, laid out after the fashion of an English park. The place suffered considerable damage during the Mutiny at the hands of the rebels, but this was subsequently repaired, and the house is now very much as it was when originally constructed.

Mr. Routledge, the first collector of the district, and to the north of the Bagladah are the old police lines, which have recently been made over to the Salvation Army, a Christian missionary by Fredrick Booth-Tucker, to be used as a Dom settlement with the object of attempting the reclamation of the Magahiyas. To the east of Basantpur is Halseyganj. The bazar is a municipal property and is named after Mr. Halsey, who was once an assistant magistrate of Gorakhpur.

The Urdu bazar to the north east of Halseyganj is the chief business centre of the town. The eastern side of the mohalla is where the dispensary, Dufferin hospital, as well as the campier hall is present. The last is a handsome structure in Oriental style, built from a fund of 10000 rupees left by Mr JB Campier to be used for the erection of a hall to commemorate his father.

In front of the hall stands a bronze statue of her late, majestic Queen Victoria, recently crowned with a white marble canopy. Since its completion in 1900, the hall has been used as an office for the municipal board, which has its meeting here, and also serves as a courthouse for the bench of honorary magistrates, which is utilised for public meetings when the occasion arises. To the west of Mia Bazar is the Nakhas Mohalla,which is the Kotwali or central police station, and to the north-west are the Jubilee High School and the Gorakhpur Bank. To the south of the Campier Hall are the telegraph office and the magistrate's lock-up, while south again of these is the large dharmsala built in 1837 by Mr. Reade, the Commissioner of Gorakhpur. It is surrounded by a castellated wall with a tower over the entrance gate, and is under the management of the district board. Mention should also be made of the Government normal school, situated in the south of the town in the compound which formerly belonged to Mr. Bridgman, the grantee of the Lehra estate.

The notified area to the east of the municipality contains the civil station, the old cantonment, and several villages to the south and east. The magistrate's office, the police office, the treasury, the fine new record room, and the tahsil buildings form a compact group on an open space opposite the Campier Hall. Immediately to the south is the English church, which stands in a corner of the large compound belonging to the Church Missionary Society. The latter also contains, in addition to the two houses of the missionaries, a small Christian colony. Further cast, beyond the dak bungalow, is a substantial building in red brick, containing the commissioner's court and office; while joining it are the courts of the sessions and subordinate judges and the bar library. To the north of this wore the infantry lines of former days, in the trees to the cast of the club house; to the east of these is the parade ground; but the sole remaining belonging of the old military station, save for a few outhouses , is the hospital, now used as the mess of the Gorakhpur squadron of the United Provinces Horse. In the north-east of the notified area stands the Gurkha dharmsala, built for the benefit of pensioners and other visitors from Nepal. South of this is the old Gurkha recruiting depôt, at present serving as temporary police lines; for owing to the rapidly growing importance of Gorakhpur as a recruiting centre, a new depôt is to be constructed beyond the bridge over the arm of the Ramgarh Tal on the road to Kasin. In the eastern extremity of the notified area is the racecourse, and south of this is the Hoey Park, laid out by Mr. Hoey for the use of the residents of the town and the civil station and opened by Sir Charles Crosthwaite in 1894. The cost was met from public subscriptions, and for its maintenance, there is an endowment held in trust by the collector.

To the north of the notified area is the railway station, standing in a large plot of land, which extends on either side of the line, belonging to the railway company. The size and importance of the settlement have greatly increased since the selection

Citation - H.R NEVILL GAZETTEER, 1909

Theosophical Lodge

Theosophy has developed alongside human society, making its origins deeply rooted in ancient history. The International Theosophical Society was formally established in New York on 17 November 1875 and later shifted its headquarters to the serene surroundings of Adyar, Madras. Prominent personalities such as Madam H. P. Blavatsky and Colonel H. S. Olcott received valuable support from distinguished Indian leaders, including

Dadabhai Naoroji, A. D. Hume, Surendranath Banerjee, Dr. Annie Besant, Motilal Nehru, and Swami Dayanand Saraswati in strengthening the movement.

In the early months of 1883, Colonel Olcott journeyed on horseback from Barabanki to Gorakhpur, where he convened a gathering of scholars and thinkers to promote the establishment of a local Theosophical institution. This initiative led to the founding of the Sarvahitkari Theosophical Lodge on 7 June 1883. Following this, Colonel Olcott proceeded towards Tibet. Since the Lodge initially lacked its own premises, its activities were conducted at the residence of Miss Forster.

After Miss Forster's demise in 1922, she bequeathed her entire property—including land, house, and a valuable library—to the Lodge. During her lifetime, she had also laid the foundation for the first girls' school in Gorakhpur under the banner of Theosophy. Under the leadership of Miss Barpute, the institution later progressed into a girls' high school. However, due to financial difficulties, the school was eventually taken over by the government and is presently known as A.D. Kanya Inter College, named in honor of the then president of the Lodge, Ayodhya Das.

With the assistance of the then Commissioner of Gorakhpur, Mr. Hussain, the Lodge obtained land on lease. A permanent building was later constructed on this land, dedicated to Miss Forster, under the guidance of Kunwar Bahadur, Baba Raghavdas, and Ayodhya Das. The Lodge attracted many eminent members over time, including Miss Mary, Rai Bahadur Ram Garib Lal, H. N. Wilkinson, Narsingh Prasad, Ishwari Prasad, Raja Sarju Prasad, Raja Ramnarayan Singh, Justice Vindhyavasini Prasad, Rai Krishna Kishore, Syed Abdul Bari, Madhusudan Das, Abhay Charan, Shivkumar Shastri, and Dr. K. N. Lahiri.

The Lodge actively engages in spiritual, educational, social, intellectual, and physical development initiatives. Weekly meetings are organized every Wednesday, where diverse subjects are discussed, such as the evolution of human consciousness, Narada Bhakti Sutras, Karma Yoga, Jnana Yoga and Bhakti Yoga as explained in the Bhagavad Gita, along with discussions on Buddhism, Jainism, Islam, the significance of Namaz, Christianity, the Baha'i Faith, Theosophy, devotion in the Ramcharitmanas, universal brotherhood, and nano-science. The Lodge also maintains a library containing approximately 5,000 books and operates a school aimed at educating underprivileged children. At present, S. B. R. Mishra serves as the President of the Lodge.

Citation from the book "Shaharnama Gorakhpur"

Bible Nurseries Fellowship

The Bible Fellowship Centre is situated near the roundabout adjacent to the Gorakhpur University. It belongs to the Gorakhpur Nurseries Fellowship and occupies a vast area. The centre includes a place of worship for the Christian community, where followers of Jesus Christ assemble daily for Bible readings and prayer sessions during both morning and evening hours. It is also associated with the Believers Church organization, which conducts various welfare activities from this location, including the free distribution of natural water purification systems in rural regions and providing assistance to persons with disabilities.

Citation from the book "Shaharnama Gorakhpur

Golf Ground

The Golf Ground dates back to the British period, although the exact year of its establishment is not clearly documented. It was developed primarily to cater to the recreational interests of British officials, who were particularly enthusiastic about the game of golf.

Citation from the book "Shaharnama Gorakhpur"

Pereira House

The official residence of the Vice-Chancellor of the University, commonly referred to as the "VC Lodge," was originally known as Pereira House. It once served as the private residence of Mr. Pereira, an English landlord. When academic activities commenced at the University in 1957, there was no designated accommodation for the Vice-Chancellor. Through the efforts of the University's first Vice-Chancellor, Shri Bhairavnath Jha, Pereira House was acquired during 1958–59. The building was subsequently renovated and converted into the official Vice-Chancellor's residence. Before moving into this house, Shri Bhairavnath Jha resided in the General Manager's residence of the North Eastern Railway, located in the Officers' Colony near the Railway Golf Course.

Citation from the book "Shaharnama Gorakhpur"

Theatres

The first theatre in Gorakhpur was established by Purushottam Das (Chakku Bhai) and Ramadas in the year 1924. It was named Krishna Cinema.Later, a new hall, Regent Talkies, was added. It was inaugurated in the year 1937.

Hotel

There is not much information available about the hotels.

But there was a Reade sahab ki dharmshala, which was of Mr. EA Reade, the then Collector.

It was later converted into an accommodation for the common travelers as a 'Rainbasera'.

Another was the Bombay Hotel on Venus Road.

The letter of Jennifer was written to Mr. and Mrs. Beavis at this hotel (1955).

Reade Sahab ki Dharmshala

The Reade Sahib Dharamshala, located near Betiahata Chowk, is an excellent example of Mughal-era architecture. It was built in 1680 by Qazi Khalilur Rahman, the Chakledar (revenue collector) of Gorakhpur, as a fort to house military commanders. However, its condition has deteriorated considerably. Only a few walls and some doors with their frames remain as remnants of its original craftsmanship.

In 1839, Edward Anderton Reade, the then Collector of Gorakhpur, transformed the fort into a guesthouse (Dharamshala) by collecting donations of Rs. 5880 from the local gentry and merchants. According to information from the municipal corporation, in 1836, the then District Magistrate, Mr. Reade, acquired the land from Dildar Khan through a lease deed and established a trust to build the guesthouse. The government recognized this trust through its letter number 3633 on August 17, 1844, and entrusted its management to the local body.

St. Andrew's College

With my heart beating fast and curiosity extended to the utmost, I landed up in the portals of St. Andrew's College on July 14, 1919, for my admission to the Inter, Ist year Arts. It was entirely a different world into which I had stepped. I had passed the High School Examination from the Government Jubilee High School that year, an institution which was not only the best in the station but one of the very best in the whole of the State. Sri Aghore Nath Chatterjee, who was one of the most outstanding figures in the educational world in those days, with a handsome and commanding personality, a strict disciplinarian, a high-class educationist, he had added lustre and stature to this school. The students of the Government Jubilee High School were looked upon by their local compatriots with some awe and were always rated highly.

Tracing back to the history of St Andrews, it was established as a school in 1828. Later, in 1899, it was raised to a college Raja of Tamkuhi had made a subscription to the establishment.

St. Andrew's College was teaching till the Intermediate standard with Mr. Kennedy as its principal. It became a Degree College in 1916, when it moved up to the present building. Mr. Garfield Williams, who was the Principal of this College and a renowned Anglican priest, was later awarded the Order of the British Empire, which had pulled the college into great prominence. Mr. Zakir Husain, one of the first graduates of this college, was appointed as a Deputy Collector in 1918. This gave considerable fillip to the status of this college. But Mr Garfield had left towards the end of 1918 for a more important job in the Government, and had been succeeded by the tall, thin, blue-eyed, honest, and deeply religious Mr. A.C. Pelly as Principal.

Mr. Pelly was from Wickham and had married Ms. Emily Stern, daughter of the C.M.S Missionary Rev. Henry Stern.

Arrival of Mahatma Gandhi

During the four years that I was in the Jubilee School and at the St. Andrew's College, some important social and political events took place, which exercised our minds to the utmost. The first thing was the Sharda Bill advocating Inter-caste marriage. An educated society was divided on this question, and frequent public meetings were held in support of this measure, some of which were badly disturbed. I remember in one meeting held in the Town Hall, Shri Nihar Kumar Sanyal, then a young legal practitioner, who got up to support the measure, was not allowed to speak, so great was the hooting and howling. But he stood undaunted and resolute at the platform and said he would have his say. This unseemly controversy went on for weeks, and telegrams on behalf of the public were sent to the Imperial Legislative Council both in support of and against the measure. I used to attend all the meetings and was against the bill, which appears to have been dropped later.The second phenomenon was the Home Rule agitation started by Mrs. Annie Besant. Munshi Ishwar Saran used to address weekly meetings on Home Rule, and I never missed them. He had an impressive personality and was a fine speaker. His meetings were usually well attended,

But all those faded into insignificance before the stormy non-cooperation movement launched by Gandhiji. This was first heralded by protest meetings and nationwide fasts against the Jallianwala Bagh atrocity. The student world was particularly agitated over it. Later on, Mahatma Gandhi announced his non-cooperation movement programme. Mahatma Gandhi paid a visit to Gorakhpur in February 1921, when a mammoth meeting attended by about two lakh people was held in Bale-ka Maidan. A large volunteer corps had been organized by B. Raghupati Sahai, who had given up his appointment as a Deputy Collector in response to the call of non-cooperation. I, along with a large number of students, had joined this corps. I was one of the fifty volunteers who were to escort Mahatmaji from the Railway train to the waiting coach. But the crowd was so large and pressed forward so heavily to have a Darshan of the Great Mahatma that as soon as he alighted from the train, the double cordon of the student volunteers broke down and Mahatma was in danger of being crushed, had not the stalwart Ali Brothers, and the broad chested Dr. Bridge, the Vice Principal of our College (St. Andrew's) stepped in to form a new cordon and stop the surging crowd. The student volunteers were helpless to do their duty. I was just pushed out of the platform and was carried aloft by the crowd for a few yards, and was in fear of being dropped on the ground and being trampled down to death by the milling crowd, but the crowd was so thick and dense that there was no space where one could fall on the ground. How I saved myself is a miracle.

With nerves completely shattered, I hastened to the residence of B. Saraswati Prasad Vakil, where the Mahatma was staying, and was asked to mount guard on the room where Mahatmaji was staying. No one was permitted to enter the room without my permission.After Mahatmaji had met people and had taken his day meals, he took a little rest and then drove to Baleka Maidan, where a vast concourse of people had gathered from far-off places to have a look at a man who had been so bold as to defy the mighty British Empire.

There were a number of rumours afloat regarding danger to Mahatma Gandhi's life. One important rumour was that Mr. A.P Collect, I.C.S, the then Collector of Gorakhpur, had decided to shoot down the Mahatma when he was to pass in a procession by the post office. There were other rumours that some European indigo planters or farmers would shoot him down. Baseless, as these rumours proved to be, they exercised everybody's mind greatly, and everybody was apprehensive that something might take place. But nothing happened, and this further heightened the prestige of Mahatmaji.

In the meeting, Mahatmaji spoke in his feeble voice and broken Hindi. There was no logic or sentimentality in the speech. It was not an impressive speech. As against this, Maulana Mohammad Ali made an impassioned and powerful speech, which was full of rhetoric, logic, facts, and arguments, and made the best impression on our young minds. Shaukat Ali also spoke, but he had neither the personality of the Mahatma nor the brilliance of Mohammad Ali.

The meeting ended, and people dispersed with regret. Mahatma Gandhi left by the 8 p.m. train. I was privileged to be with him all through till he left, a rare privilege for a student of the Inter class, all due to B. Saraswati Prasad, the host, who had a great regard for me, and who knew me intimately as I was the Honorary General Secretary of the Hindu Chhatra Sabha of which he was the President for a long time.

But this visit and the departure of the Mahatma threw up new problems for me. Babu Raghupati Sahai had exhorted the student volunteers to leave off their studies in fulfillment of the seven items of the Non-Cooperation movement, and to make the declaration coincide with Mahatma's visit. Most of my friends expected me to take the lead. The announcement could not be made on the day of the visit, as all thought was concentrated on the visit itself. A matter of educational attainment. He asked me what my intentions were.

I told him that I intended to take the examination, but I was helpless as my friends and associates did not leave me any time. I told him that 1 fully realised that, if I of non-cooperation after my failure, it would take the edge off the announcement, but I saw no way out. He then suggested that I had, in that case, better leave that very night for my village, where I should prepare for my examination, as preparation leave had already been given to us, and there would not be any loss of attendance. I was not likely to be bothered in my village by my friends.

I clutched at that advice, as a drowning man caught at a straw, and left for my village, by the midnight train with all my books, bedding, and belongings, where I reached the next morning with a coolie carrying all my belongings. My 3rd brother, Pt. Agardi Mani Tripathi, on seeing me arrive with all my luggage, thought that I had left my studies in response to Mahatma Gandhi's call and had come away with my things. He felt annoyed and asked me how I had come away from Gorakhpur on the eve of my examination. I told him that, as other fellow students constantly disturbed me and would not allow me to continue my studies, I had come home to prepare for my examination. As he was a man of very strong will and determination, and as he knew of my part in Mahatma's visit, he did not believe me and told me that nobody could disturb one who was determined to continue his studies, and that if it was true that I wanted to prepare for my examination and did not want to non-cooperate I had better return to Gorakhpur and stay there and prepare for my examination. It was due to the intervention of my eldest brother that he allowed me to remain for the day at home, but sent me away the next morning.

When my friends came to meet me the next day of my departure from my residence in Gorakhpur, they were told that I had left for home. They were surprised, and some interpreted my departure as non-cooperation, and others as a flight from an embarrassing situation. Anyway, they ceased coming to my house, and when I arrived at

Gorakhpur the third day, I had a comparatively quiet time. I had barely 20 days to prepare for my examination, having wasted over a month in the preparation for Mahatma's visit, and a week in deciding what to do.

I tried to work hard, but shortly after, I developed some eye trouble. I, however, managed to appear and pass my Inter examination to the great relief of my brother. About half a dozen students gave up their studies.

Most of them were those who did not expect to pass their examinations. Only one, B. Gaya Prasad, who was a good student and who expected to do well, made a real sacrifice and did not appear at the Inter Examination. He had to regret his decision and later on entered railway service in a humble position, but being intelligent and industrious made up some of the lost ground. But had he not non-cooperated, he would have done exceedingly well in life.

Arrival of Queen Elizabeth in Gorakhpur

Queen Elizabeth II of Britain passed away at the age of 96 at Balmoral Castle in Scotland on September 8th. Countries around the world are mourning the Queen's death. Interestingly, Queen Elizabeth visited Gorakhpur in the 1950s. The Majithia royal family of Sardar Nagar welcomed her. Sukhdev Singh Majithia recounted that a special room was set up at the airport for Queen Elizabeth in 1950. According to him, the Queen's plane was running low on fuel, and it was immediately diverted to Gorakhpur airport, where she was welcomed by Sardar Surinder Singh Majithia. Sukhdev also shared with us that the Queen had bestowed upon him the title of knighthood. She had also conferred the title of "Sir" on

Surjit Singh Majithia, who was the Defense Minister at the time. Dr. Egan's daughter, Juliet, told me over the phone that Sardar Dalip Singh Majithia had also served in the Indian Air Force. After retiring and returning to Gorakhpur to pursue his passion for flying, he not only bought a chartered plane but also built an airport, which is now known as Gorakhpur Airport.

The Chauri Chaura Incident

On February 4, 1922, a group of non-cooperation movement participants clashed with local authorities, attacked police officers, and burnt the police station, which unfortunately led to the death of 22 police officers and 3 civilians.

The incident occurred at Chauri Chaura in Gorakhpur 2nd of September 1920, Mahatma Gandhi introduced the non-cooperation movement, which was assumed to be a non-violent corporation. We are people who gave up their government titles and jobs.

On February 4, about 5,000 people gathered in the village of Dumri and marched to the police station in Chauri Chaura. Among the protesters was Sampat Das. From a distance, his 14- year-old nephew Savaro stood and watched the drama with excitement as the crowd approached the police station. Today, Savaro Das is over 80, but he clearly remembers that fateful February dayThe protest leaders went inside to discuss the earlier beating with the police chief. Singh, who had just been reinforced by police from Gorakhpur, laughed in the protesters' faces and ordered his men to disperse the crowd. But that was easier said than done. Instead of dispersing the gathering, people began throwing stones, collected from the nearby railway embankment, at the police station. "Mahatma Gandhi ki jay," the crowd chanted, "hail to the great spirit Gandhi." The police opened fire, but at first only fired warning shots into the air.

Savaro Das says that people were amazed that no one was injured by the gunfire. The courage of the volunteers grew. Although they chanted Gandhi's name, they had forgotten his call for non-violence and pushed forward towards the police station with stones flying from their hands. Shocked by the seriousness of the situation, the police chief ordered his men to shoot to kill.

Three people lost their lives in the gunfire, but the police were so badly attacked by the stone-throwers that they were forced to take cover inside the police station.

Do you know who the first PCS officer of Uttar Pradesh was?

Yes, it was Dr. Shruti Narayan Mani Tripathi. A personality who was an inspiration for every student of Purvanchal in the early 1900s. S.N.M. Tripathi was born in 1900 in

Barpar, Deoria. He completed his schooling at Majhauli and Sirjam. After that, he enrolled in St. Andrew's College, Gorakhpur, for his graduation. Getting college admission was very difficult at that time. But S.N.M. Tripathi's dedication led him to pursue a doctorate (PhD) from Muir Central College, Allahabad. After completing his education, he returned to Gorakhpur to practice law in the district court. While working, he was preparing for the civil services and finally cleared the exam in 1925. After training, his first posting was in Basti.

Anecdote - After receiving this information, I went to S.N.M. Tripathi's residence in Civil Lines to gather some more information, where I met his nephew, Dr. Shukla. He was a retired professor of Botany from Balrampur Degree College. He told me many new things about S.N.M. Tripathi. Gorakhpur University or DDU was established based on his idea, and he was a key founding member of this institution. He had a very strict attitude towards European collectors and the British government. One story told by Dr. Shukla was that once, on the arrival of the King of England, celebrations were announced throughout the country. All district collectors were ordered to take out processions in their respective districts. And S.N.M. Tripathi was the Collector of Sultanpur at that time, so while leading the procession, the crowd asked him to burst some firecrackers, which he readily agreed to. The crowd started bursting firecrackers, and suddenly, the European Superintendent of Police's horse got frightened and started jumping, causing it to fall. They were very angry and complained about the incident to the Commissioner. The Commissioner summoned S.N.M. Tripathi. He replied to the Commissioner by saying that an SP who cannot control his own horse, how can he control a crowd? This story in itself reflects the qualities and personality of Tripathi ji.

Shri Shukla also mentioned that his father was a farmer and came from a typical middle-class family. S.N.M. Tripathi's son, Lieutenant General Prakash Mani Tripathi, was a Member of Parliament from Deoria, and his grandson, Shashank Mani Tripathi (an alumnus of IIT Delhi), is currently the Member of Parliament from the same constituency.

Dr. S.N.M. Tripathi's autobiography depicts several significant events related to the history of Uttar Pradesh. Some of them include Gandhiji's arrival in Gorakhpur, the conflict with Shibban Lal Saxena, Sardar Nagar, Kanpur, Allahabad, and much more...

It was Shruti Narayan Mani Tripathi who proved that with confidence, even mountains can be moved. In a country that was a colony of the British Empire and where Indians were discriminated against in government service, he overcame all challenges and became a source of inspiration for the people of Purvanchal.

Narrative of S.N.M Tripathi

I joined the college, except for a few friends and classmates who joined the college with me, I knew very few of the older boys. The first shock came when we were required to speak in When English not only inside and outside classrooms, but throughout our stay, within the college and its premises. The boys of those days, unlike the boys of today who passed out of High School, could speak in English, but were not used to conversing in English freely, and to express all kinds of thoughts in that language. This at once gave us a rude jolt and made us feel inferior to our seniors, who had gotten used to speaking in English. This, however, gave us a sense of importance, and we felt that we now belonged to a class that was lifted above the average citizen.

Another thing that added importance to our lives was putting on black gowns, which was compulsory for all the students. We had, during our school career, on occasions, strayed into law courts, and found that the sessions judge and the lawyers appearing before him had to put on gowns which made them look impressive and important. With these ideas in our minds, we felt important when we put on our gowns, which also gave us a feeling of manhood.

The third important difference between school and college life was the choice of subjects. During our school days, we had no choice of subjects, but here we not only had the option to choose certain subjects but found that we could take subjects like Logic and Philosophy, which opened up new branches of knowledge to us.

Fourthly, we were given much wider facilities for borrowing books from the library, and were allowed to sit and read them in the library, which was in complete contrast to the libraries and the rules of borrowing books from the school libraries. For the first time, we found a well-stocked and well-arranged library with a room for sitting and reading. Newly acquired, well-bound, shining volumes attracted us by their very appearance and invoked a desire to possess them, and once we got them, curiosity led us further to look into them. This, for the first time, showed us that there were a vast number of subjects on which a vast number of books were available and that one could devote his time and leisure to studying them.

Fifthly, we were freed from the task of preparing our daily lessons and answering questions in the classroom every day. This gave us great mental freedom, and gave us a sense of responsibility and trustworthiness.

Lastly, we had more time and freedom for study. Sometimes classes were over by 2 p.m, and sometimes by 3 p.m., so we got home rather early and had more time and leisure and a better atmosphere conducive to study. This whipped up our desire to acquire better knowledge.

I offered Sanskrit, History, and Logic as optional subjects besides English, which was not only compulsory, but everything was heavily weighted in its favour. English used to be taught by Shri A.C. Pelly, the Principal, Shri A.C. Chatterjee, Shri Thomas, and Shri B.C. Mukerjee.

English being his mother tongue, Mr. A.C. Pelly who taught us poetry, was treated with great awe and reverence, But to an English man many points, which appeared difficult for an Indian student, did not strike as calling for any explanation and, even though we found that we had certain difficulties, we were afraid to ask questions for fear of giving an impression that we were below the average level of the class.

My stay in the college lasted only two years, as I joined the first year B. A. in the Muir Central College, Allahabad in July 1921. Life was more placid and less exciting then. There were no unions, no demands by students, no hooting of teachers, no strikes, and no disturbances. There were no problems with discipline. Educational institutions were treated as very sacred places and places of learning. The ambitions of students of those days were either to distinguish themselves in sports and on the playground or in their studies. The students of those days looked upon their elders, their teachers, and even their senior students with respect and never took any kind of liberties with them.

Legal

The court in Gorakhpur district was established around 1890. At that time, there was only one English judge, and a single magistrate and a single Munsif handled all criminal and civil cases. Court proceedings were conducted in Urdu and English. Lawyers were available to assist the litigants. At that time, there were only 4-6 lawyers, who were referred to as "Vakil Saheb" (respected lawyer).

The Bar Association of the Civil Court was formally constituted in 1895, and its first meeting was held on October 18, 1895, under the chairmanship of Munshi Haridutt, a lawyer. Among the lawyers who were highly respected at that time and whose careers spanned from 1900 to 1920, Munshi Narsingh Prasad and Babu Chhotu Lal were prominent. They earned great renown.

Babu Chhotu Lal had two sons: Babu Ishwar Sharan Srivastava and Babu Shambhu Sharan Srivastava. Babu Shambhu Sharan Srivastava was sent to England to obtain a barrister's degree. He returned to Gorakhpur after receiving his Bar-at-Law degree and began practicing law there. From 1920 to 1950, he served the public in the criminal courts and maintained his influence until 1950.

Narrative of S.N.M Tripathi (1925)

It was on July 3, 1925, that one joined the Gorakhpur Bar as a Vakil enrolled in the Gorakhpur Judgeship. My L.L.B. results were out by about the 1st week of June 1925, and 1 applied immediately to be enrolled as a lawyer in the Gorakhpur Judgeship. Unlike these days, High Court orders used to be received within days, and I was enrolled before the Civil Courts on July 3, 1925.

I thus stepped into the Bar as a full-fledged lawyer. On the very first day, I was privileged to file five civil suits on my own without any help or guidance from anyone except my Moharrir, who was a very clever and able man.

My great dream of becoming a Vakil, which I had entertained since boyhood, had come to be realised, and I was in my element at the bar. I had often attended various kinds of courts during my student days with my brothers and other relatives. During my years as a student, I was sometimes asked by my eldest brother to go and do ,a pair of our family cases. Courts were thus not new to me, nor the lawyer class, some of whom I knew intimately since the Chhatra Sabha days. I had, therefore, gotten over the initial shyness before I became a member of the Gorakhpur Bar. And yet after entering the bar one felt as a pygmy as the Bar of Gorakhpur of those days had a galaxy of brilliant and province-wide famous lawyers like Sarvasri C.C. Dass popularly known as Charu Babu a middle-sized, handsome man with his big bulging eyes, Rai Bahadur B. Narsingh Prasad, before whom the average man quivered, Khan Bahadur, Mohammad Ismail, a very handsome man who was universally respected and liked, Babu Ayodhya Das, Bar at Law, a liberal politician and public man, Babu Saraswati Prasad, Babu Oudh Behari Lal, J. Jagdamba Prasad, Babu Gur Prasad and a number of others.

For a new entrant, whatever his previous experience, these stalwarts were enough to inspire a sense of awe and fear. But they also allowed a young lawyer not only to learn their ways and methods, but also to have them as his role models and work up to get their status and stature. Sometimes one got a chance to work with them, and that gave a glimpse of their ways of working. Shri C.C. Dass towered over everybody else, and not only did he not spare his juniors but also did not spare himself, despite his bad health. His method of working was unique. He had a private digest of his own and on that account scored over others who could use only published digests. Kai Bahadur Narsirigh Prasad was drawn from an aristocratic stock. Khan Bahadur Mohd Ismail was sparkling, brilliant, pleasant, and most vivacious. There were others, too, good in many respects. It was a privilege to be their contemporary, even though being far junior to them.

I did not stay long in the profession. But during the short period I was there, I had a good time, and very good opportunities to learn and do work. There was hardly a day that I did not get some new work. I started as a civil lawyer and knew nothing of revenue and criminal laws. But I soon got a chance to work before the Commissioners and got some very important and sensational criminal cases to do single-handedly at Kasia and Deoria. These were forgery and bribery cases, and though I was engaged as a junior in those cases, because of certain favourable orders that I was able to secure in favour of my clients, which the seniors had failed to obtain, the seniors were taken off, and I was put in charge. This was an embarrassing but highly gratifying situation for a junior like me, as it was a great event in the life of a junior to go from Gorakhpur to Kasia and Deoria to handle such important cases independently.

At the bar, I felt I was in my elements and was fast gathering a good and paying practice. But I was very sensitive and could not stand losing a case, a quality that is fatal for the mental peace of a lawyer. My rapid success in this short time was not looked upon with favour by some of the seniors. Then I was always haunted by a fear based on the career of Shri Ayodhya Das, Bar-at-Law, that some situation may develop in which I might lose my practice and position, even if I was able to achieve a tolerably good practice at the bar. But my career at the bar was cut short as in December 1925, the result of the competitive examination for P.C.S. was announced, in which I got one place out of the four allotted to non-muslims.

But this led to a few remonstrations from some of my friends and some of the Civil Court officers who regretted my decision to join the service. One of the Muslim Judicial Officers, on hearing of my success in the examination, came to my house one evening and said that he had come to condole with me. I was startled and asked him, "What for?" "On your success at the PCS examination," he said. I said this was a matter of congratulations rather than an expression of sorrow. He said he was sorry both for me and for the Gorakhpur Bar. He said I had ruined my career, as in five years I would have beaten the top man of the Gorakhpur Bar. This was too tall a praise, and I began to wonder whether I was imagining it all. I told him that this was undeserved praise. He replied that he had no reason to flatter me But this was not the solitary case. I met a Vakil of Bihar travelling by bus from Kasia to Deoria when I was coming to Deoria after having argued a forgery and bribery case before a Magistrate in Kasia. This Vakil was present in court throughout and heard my arguments. When we met on the bus, during the course of our talk, he learnt that I had successfully cleared the P.C.S examination and intended to leave the profession. He was taken aback and, paying very high tribute, said that I would "rue my decision to join service". He said I was cut out for the bar and that if nothing untoward happened would scale great heights in this profession Though, these were extraordinary certificates for a lawyer of six months standing and though they gave me some confidence, for reasons which had the appearance of compulsion I gave up my practice at the bar in April 1926 with many pleasant memories, and considerable amount of regret as I had to exchange a free life for the life in Government service.

Railways

Gorakhpur Railway Station 1890

The development of any region depends on the infrastructure available there. Until the 1880s, the Rapti River was a major source of goods transportation in Gorakhpur and the surrounding areas. Goods were primarily transported by waterways, with Barhaj serving as a central hub. In the early 1880s, the prospect of railway development emerged, becoming a reality in 1885. The Bengal North Western Railway opened a 220.47-mile-long meter-gauge railway line from Sonpur to Mankapur via Chhapra-Gorakhpur for passenger traffic on January 15, 1885.

The Gorakhpur railway station was constructed at this time. Initially, it was a single-story building with half a dozen rooms. A signaling system with a four-lever frame, in its rudimentary stage, was located in front of the station master's office, and a refreshment room was situated at the eastern end of the platform. An agent's (General Manager's) bungalow and a loco superintendent's bungalow were also built. With the establishment of the railway network in the Gorakhpur region, the pace of development accelerated. The Gorakhpur-Uska Bazar meter-gauge railway section was constructed in 1886, and the Gorakhpur-Chhitauni section in 1907. Over time, the Gorakhpur railway station continued to develop. In 1943, the Gorakhpur railway area came under the 'Awadh Tirhut Railway'.

With the establishment of the railway in Gorakhpur, a printing press was also provided, and the railway press was transferred from Muzaffarpur to Gorakhpur in 1884. Later, in 1906, a mechanical workshop was established for the maintenance of locomotives and coaches, and it was named the 'Bengal and Assam North Western Railway Loco Carriage Workshop'. Skilled craftsmen were brought in from Samastipur. In 1947, a bridge workshop was opened within the mechanical workshop, which was later established as a signal factory in Gorakhpur Cantonment in 1954 with 20 workers.

The Railways were dominated by the Anglo Indian community.

The Railway museum stands in a bungalow (known as bungalow no. 5) which was established in 1890-1900 by the Bengal North Western railways

The Excavation at Piprawaha, Birdpur.

Mr. Peppe of Birdpur

William Claxton Peppé was born in India in 1852, his father being an estate manager in Northern India. He was educated in Aberdeen but returned to Birdpur, India, to assist his father in 1873, becoming the manager in the early 1880s. In the spring of 1897, Peppé began to excavate a mound near the village of Piprahwa on the Birdpur estate. After weeks spent clearing away soil and dense scrub that covered the mound, preliminary excavations exposed a solid mass of red fired brickwork that, after further digging, revealed itself to be a large dome roof roughly 130 feet in diameter. Peppé contacted Vincent Smith, an authority on ancient Indian history and archaeology, who decided that it was an unusually early example of an ancient Buddhist stupa, probably dating from the era of Ashoka the Great.

Excavations continued in 1898, and after digging through eighteen feet of brickwork, he found a huge slab of stone, the cover of an enormous stone coffer. Within the coffer were five vessels, none more than seven inches in height, containing quantities of stars in silver and gold, discs of gold leaf embossed with Buddhist symbols, numerous pearls of many sizes, drilled beads, stars, and flowers cut in red or white cornelian, amethyst, topaz, garnet, coral, and crystal. Also found inside the vessels were small pieces of bone and ash, and on the side of one of them, in an ancient Pali character, was an inscription that read:

"This shrine for relics of the Buddha, the August One, is that of the Sakya's, the brethren of the Distinguished One, in association with their sisters, and with their children and their wives."

William Peppé had seemingly unearthed one of the original eight stupas that were said to contain the ashes and bone fragments of the Buddha that were shared out after his cremation.

Within a week of the discovery, a Siamese Buddhist monk, Jinavaravansa, who was the grandson of King Rama III of Siam, arrived to ask that the relics go to his country. Peppé had already placed the relics at the disposal of the Government, but he sent the request to Mr. Hoey, the Commissioner of Gorakhpur. The British authorities agreed that some should be sent to Siam, other portions also went to the Museum in Kolkata, and to Colombo, Sri Lanka. Peppé was apportioned about one-sixth of the jewels.

Peppé retired from his post in 1903, returning to England, but returned to India from 1920 to 1926, before finally retiring. He died in 1936.

A Railway Mail Van Dacoity

B.N Lahiri

At about 8-30 on the evening of March 24, 1942, the UP Mail of the B.N.W.R. (now known as N.E.R.) suddenly came to a halt some two miles beyond Shahjanwa railway station. For a while, all was quiet, and the passengers wondered what the matter could be. Presently, some reports of a gun were heard, and these were followed by shouts of 'Bande Matarani, 'Inqolab Zindabad', 'Mahatma Gandhi ki Jai' 'Subhash Babu hi jai.' and so on. A man with a sola hat walking up and down by the side of the train along its entire length was seen distributing leaflets purporting to have been published by the Hindustan Socialist Republican Army of India, while a few of his companions kept on threatening the passengers with dire consequences if any of them attempted to offer resistance. They, moreover, announced in a loud voice that they were revolutionaries. They intended to rob the Government of the day for robbing the poor kisans and mazdoors and wanted the public to combine in overthrowing it. The Army, the Police, and the Civic Guards, they declared, were ready to shake off the foreign yoke.

Though the train was full, yet none of the passengers could pick up enough courage to fight the intruders. The latter, on their part, pulled the engine driver out and made him sit in a first-class compartment by the side of a travelling ticket collector. Likewise, they kept the Guard and the Assistant Guard under detention in another first-class compartment. Thereafter, some of them went over to the mail van, gained forcible entry into it, after breaking open its glass windows, and rifled all the insured covers and cash available. to the value of approximately Rs. 10,000. Throughout the proceedings, which lasted for some fortyfive minutes, the assailants had it all their own way. But it must be said to their credit that they did not manhandle anyone nor did they tamper with any personal property. Having thus gained their object, they collected at one spot when their leader took fatally of their number before they marched off in a body to disappear into the darkness along with their booty. Information about this outrage was first received by the police Station Shahjanwa through the Village Chaukidar. The Station Officer Shahjanwa flashed the news to Mr. Luck, Superintendent of Police at Gorakhpur, who arrived at the scene with the greatest despatch. But since the train had in the meantime left for the next station, that is, Magahar, he went over there and held a full enquiry. Having done this, he had the mail van detached and hauled back to Gorakhpur after some time. According to eyewitnesses, the intruders were all young men. looked like students and wore an assortment of hats, turbans, dhoties, pyjamas, and trousers. Most of them had handkerchiefs tied round their faces to hide their identity. One unexploded and five exploded crackers were found at the spot, apart from one 22 bore rook rifle bolt.

This was all the clue to be had. But by all appearances-ces,here was a case of no ordinary type. One marked feature of it was that the culprits—one and all—appeared to be educated young men who gave themselves out as members of the H.S.R.A. Another was that they scrupulously avoided doing anything to harm the passengers. The leaflets they distributed, moreover, made no secret of their aims and objects.

The only inference, therefore, possible was that this was a case of politico-criminal dacoity committed in furtherance of a deep-laid plot to cause a severe jolt to the Government of The day, its pattern being the same as that of two other recent cases, one of Barbatpur in district Varanasi and the other of Nandganj in district Ghazipur.

Wires started jangling within a short time of the occurrence to convey the news to all quarters that might be interested in it. The U.P. administration was, at the time, being run by a caretaker Government. Their hands were already full—what with having to make an all-out effort in support of the Great World War that was going on and what with the ticklish business of running the day-to-day administration, in the face of an all-India agitation that was to culminate before long in the Quit India Movement of August 1942. To make matters worse, the fortunes of the war were then going against the Allies, thus giving rise to a state of acute nervousness in Government circles. In this context, therefore, it was but natural for the investigation of this case to be entrusted promptly to the charge of the C.I.D., who were expected to be able to work it out with much greater facility than the regular Police. This also explains my association with it.

Within a few hours of the occurrence, 1 found myself speeding on my way to Gorakhpur by car, along with my team. As soon as we got there, the first thing we did was to carry out a systematic inspection of the ill-fated Mail Van in this case.

Among the scores of torn envelopes lying about on the floor of the van, there were some with finger impressions on them, stained in blood. Similar impressions were also to be seen on a broken window pane of the van. This clearly showed that at least one of the culprits had sustained a cut on the finger in an attempt to smash open the glass window, and had left behind him these tell-tale impressions, in trying to wipe off the blood oozing from it.

Our next step was to have these fingerprints developed and then photographed by one of our experts. This done, we turned our attention to the task of tracing the man with the injured finger. Following the age-old method of working through 'sources', we soon came to know that he was one Oudhraj Tewari, of Gorakhpur. We raided his village home, we raided all his other possible haunts, but without any luck. This only meant that he had gone underground. Without giving rise to any suspicion in his mind, we then made a close study of the man's movements from such bits and pieces of information has come our way. This was a game that had its quota of thrills, its trials and tribulations. On one occasion, my Deputy Rai Bahadur Tika Ram and I, disguised as ordinary businessmen, remained hidden in a lane for almost a whole day in wait for our quarry, without being rewarded for our Pain. However, it came to be known before long that in the evenings he was in the habit of visiting on the sly a tea shop in the Gorakhpur bazar. One evening, therefore, while he was quietly sipping his tea in a dark corner of this shop,the Rai Bahadur and I swooped upon him and whisked him away to the Kotwali without attracting much notice. There we questioned him again and again, with all the skill at our command, about his complicity in the train outrage, but he persisted in vigorously pleading his innocence. One thing he could not get away with was a tell-tale injury mark on the tip of his right thumb, though he tried to explain it away, somewhat foolishly, by saying that it was a cut sustained from the sharp end of a ploughshare.

Oudhraj was not much to look at, being no more than a slim young man, aged about 22-23 years, with a dark complexion and a pockmarked face. What impressed us most about him was his grim determination not to give in to any threats or cajolery on our part to make him speak up. The only means now open to us to verify his complicity was to take his finger impressions—incidentally, not at all an easy thing to do in face of the stiff resistance he put up against it—and send them lor comparison to the Finger Print Bureau at Allahabad, iliis we did and, sure enough, they were found to tally with the blood-stained impressions detected on several torn envelopes picked up from the floor of the Mail Van in question.

Thus, so far as this man was concerned, there could not be the least doubt about his complicity in the case wc were investigating. But this was poor consolation to us, so long as the identity of the rest of the gang remained shrouded in mystery. At one stage, we seemed to have come to a dead end, seeing that except for two interesting letters in our hand—which merely went to confirm that offshoots of the H.S.R.A. in the eastern districts of Uttar Pradesh had been planning a 'money action' for some time—we had nothing else to go upon. In one of these letters, a person who had signed himself as Bengali Babu had written to an acquaintance of his at < xorakhpur mentioning Hari Pratap Tewari. In the other one, Oullar of Allahabad had written to a man of Basti to say that he (Gullar) had been requested by a Benaras student to receive anti hide a large amount of money that the latter had planned to loot.Days, even months, passed without any development, and we had all but abandoned hope of making any further headway, when a 'source' again came to our rescue. The information he gave was that some local students of Gorakhpur, led by Hari Pratap Tewari and Indra Prasad had been experimenting with the preparation of bombs in a certain rented house in the town. This was enough to revive our drooping spirits, and we at once got busy trying to verify this information. The house in question turned out to be an unpretentious-looking building situated in a quiet corner and used as a private hostel for boys attending some of the local schools and colleges. But, unfortunately for us, we found that the birds we were after had flown away, having left for home to enjoy their summer vacations. This was disappointing. But, in spite of this initial handicap, the information we sought was verified by a number of residents. According to them, some time previously, there had been an explosion of a crude bomb that these youths had been trying to make surreptitiously. Fragments of the bomb were also found at their point of impact, lying mixed up in a refuse dump at the back of the house! Our next link in this chain of events was supplied by a resident of Azamgarh who made a statement throwing a flood of light on the activities in general of the H.S.R.A. in the eastern districts during the past few years. Following this disclosure, the names of many of the members of this Association were ascertained, and extensive searches, interrogations, and arrests were carried out. Some materials, as well as tools for the manufacture of explosives, were also recovered, along with large quantities of terrorist literature. But there was no trace to be had of Hari Pratap Tewari or of Indra Prasad or any of their associates, even.

Next followed the recovery, after some weeks, from the possession of one Ramadhar Singh, a contact of Indra Prasad, of a list containing the names of certain youths. In it there was mentioned of one Raja Ram Passi, an ex-student of the Gorakhpur High School, who was found to be absconding.

About this time, it came to be known that two students of the Queen's College at Benaras were in touch with some of the important suspects in this case. Their houses were located. A raid was carried out on November 27, when they were arrested along with three others, namely Hari Pratap Tewari of Gorakhpur, Brij Bahadur of Barabanki, and Ramji Ram Vaish of Ghazipur, all of whom had been absconding. Hari Pratap Tewari and Brij Bahadur were, moreover, found in possession of service revolvers, fully loaded. These three arrests were made by Rai Bahadur Fika Ram in somewhat dramatic circumstances. His idea was first to throw a cordon round the house and thereafter to carry out a systematic search of it, on the off chance of coming by one or other of the suspects in this case. It so happened that while he was still making his enquiries inside the house, the three very men he had been looking out for, walked in quite unsuspectingly, thus falling an easy prey into his hands! This time, luck was certainly on our side! One other suspect, Bhagwan Prasad Shukla, was arrested with a number of others on the night of

December 3 at Lucknow, following a raid carried out by Khan Sahib Nasir Khan, Deputy Superintendent of Police, Special Branch.

Almost thirty arrests had been made by now, and there was reason to believe that some of those arrested had been responsible, the previous April, for the blackening of Queen Victoria's statue in the Town Hall at Gorakhpur.

Kailash Pati, still another suspect in this case, was arrested in circumstances reflecting credit on certain members of the public. He had come to Gorakhpur to meet an associate of his. Not finding him at home, he had chosen to stay at his friend's house for the night. This aroused the suspicion of a resident, who promptly relayed the information to certain members of the Civic Guard. The latter, in their turn, took Kailash Pati to the Kotwali, where he was identified and locked up. He had been wanted in connection with both this case and a case of postal robbery of Benaras in 1939.

Raja Ram Passi, whose name found mention in a list recovered from the possession of Ramadhar Singh, surrendered himself on December 28 and gave a detailed statement, con- fessing his guilt and naming all his accomplices, except three, whom he did not know. His confession ran as follows:

There were fourteen of us. Balrup and I left Gorakhpur by the train, which was to be looted. Four others boarded it at the next station, Domingarh, while the rest were already present at the spot, where, by previous arrangement, the train was to be stopped by pulling its alarm chain.

Balrup had brought some leaflets with him which he distributed among the passengers. Bhagwan Prasad Shukla directed the operations while Baijnath Singh and Balrup collected the loot. Baijnath Singh, Unia Shanker Upadhyaya, and Balrup each had a revolver.

After the commission of the dacoity, Vidya Sahi and I returned home on a bicycle. Thereafter, about the 15th of May, Kailashpati, Balrup, and I left for a village in Nepal* territory, where we met Uma Shankar, Baijnath Singh, Rajnath Singh and Bhagwan Prasad Shukla. The following day, Uma Shankar and I left for Rewa, with six hundred rupees, for the purchase of arms. But, failing to obtain any There, we left for Gwalior, where we rented a room. Here we were joined by Chutkun Misra, Hari Pratap Tewari, Baijnath, and Balrup.

Following the record of Raja Ram Passi's statement, Rai Bahadur Tika Ram and Inspector Faizan Ullah proceeded, post-haste, to Gwalior. There, they first located the house mentioned by Raja Ram Passi and, after some time, managed to arrest Uma Shankar, Baijnath Singh, and Rajnath Singh, along with two six-chamber revolvers, a large number of cartridges, a quantity of gunpowder, and some lead.

In this way, nearly all those involved in the case came to be rounded up. Out of the two, namely, Kailashpati and Balrup, escaped from jail. Raja Ram was tendered pardon and examined as an approver. The identity of one could not be established, and two others remained at large, thus leaving a balance of eight who were all sentenced to six years R.I. by the Court of Sessions at Lucknow.

With the conviction of these accused, the curtain was rung down on a serious politico-criminal case of U.P., in the course of investigation of which much information was gleaned about the activities of a large number of youths belonging to the Eastern districts of this State, who were out to overthrow the Government of the day. Although misguided, most of them were inspired by high ideals and were prepared to suffer the worst of privations in the attainment of their objective. This was borne out by a letter written by Hari Pratap Tewari from his hide-out to his newly-wedded wife, exhorting her to live up to the glorious traditions set by the women of Chittor, and, if need be, to wipe off all memory of him from her mind. But the wheel of time has turned full circle since, and those who were dubbed as rebels then are acclaimed as heroes today!

THE EURASIANS

Have you ever heard the word Anglo Indian? This is the race that has been living in our country since the British era. Before the British invasion. The geographical exploration during the European Renaissance of the 15th century brought a new element to the Indian scene. The European settlements and conquest once again started a new wave of commingling. During Portuguese heyday, the question of a separate crossbed community did not arise. If not on temporary assignment, the French and the death of a settler in their colonies. Their interest lay "In the land of their adoption rather than in that of their birth". If we talk about the geographical planning, there was a township built in Madras known as the White town. Albarbeque did everything in his power to encourage the Portuguese to take Indian wives. Then the origin of Anglo Indians can be seen in the rival of the East India Company. Young Englishmen used to come to India for jobs, but there were no European women to marry them. So they were inclined towards the Indian women. The children born to them came to be known as Anglo Indians. It was said, "by far the greater number of actual Eurasians are either Mohammedan or the lower caste of Hindus", who did not merge into the indigenous Christian population. Owing to the social and mental habits of their father's race. It was allegedly time and again that the Anglo Indians had inherited the worst of the two worlds, India and England. Thurston and Rangchari quote the following Anglo Indian surnames:

Gomes, D'Souza, D'Costa, D'silva, D'Cruz, Gonsalves, Rozario, Labral, Fernandes, Fonseca, Lazaro, Xavier, Mendoza, Rodriguez, Saldana, Almeyda, Heldt, Vonspell, Janzon, Austine, Brisson, Cornville, Le Granze, Lavacot, Pascal, Devine, Hurbert, Ryan, McKertish, Mcpherson, besides more popular surnames like Johnson and Smith.

These include Portuguese, French, German, and English surnames, throwing sufficient light on the wideness of mixture. The same European food, English wine, and clothing going to clubs were the trends of this community.

There are some interesting, fun facts: Norman Willis, who was the manager of the Tamkuhi sugar mill, (Established by the Scottish Businessman F. Guthrie in 1925), went back to England after independence, leaving his sister Moira in India.

Mr. Boye an army officer in the Gurkha regiment, got some financial help from the company for his services rendered, Mr. George Lloyd, wing commander in the Air force left the country and went back to England along with his family.

Mr. G Yeoward of Gonda received a compensation sum of Rs. 500 for the losses suffered during the sepoy mutiny.

Gary Magnum, a state-level guitarist who used to work in a circus, resided in Dharampur.

Many of the Anglo Indians went back to England, Canada, Australia, and New Zealand in search of a better living, and a second reason was the vulnerability of living in a country that was a colony of their white forefathers. On the other hand, I have experienced that many of the Anglo Indians are suffering from poverty because of having the habit of living a laid back lifestyle, which they received during the colonial period.

Many unknown families of the community include Mcintosh, Richards, Elliott, and Sullivan.

The Cyrill family

The well-known family of the Anglo Indian community of Gorakhpur is the Cyrill family.

Mr. David Cyrill had acted as the head of the All India Anglo Indian association of Gorakhpur. If we talk about the ancestry David's grandfather was Mr. George Cyrill, who was married to Ms. Grace Winifred. Mr. George had three brothers and two sisters. One brother was a pilot in Air India. Another brother Alfred, was married to Ms. Mary Dorothy Nickels.

Nickels were the Land proprietors of Zamania, Ghazipur. Other being in the B.N.W railways.

Mr. David tells that his grandmother (Ms. Grace Winifred Cyrill) was the first appointed headmistress of the railway mixed primary school.

After retirement, she thought of opening a school to impart education through her knowledge and experience. The school has been converted into an inter-college.

Another contribution of hers is the Darbhanga College, which was started by her at the request of the then Railway Minister L.N Mishra.

David's father was Ian Anthony Cyrill, who was a manager for Indian Airlines.

David had also worked for the Cruise lines in the U.S.A for almost 7 years and then in England. He returned to Gorakhpur after leaving the job and is now the principal of St. Jude's School, which was established by his grandmother.

He is also the regional sports coordinator for the ICSE. His wife is Mrs. Charmaine Cyrill.

Mr. David's wife Charamine is from Kanpur and is of Goan- Portuguese descent. They both have three children One of the daughters is in Australia pursuing her graduation in applied finance.

An interesting anecdote enunciated by David was the midnight picnic in the jungles of Kushmi. Mr. Emile

Macedo, a dear friend of his father, used to come at 11 at night, and all the 6 members were loaded in the Fiat car. They used to go to the Budhiya Mata Mandir for a picnic, where they used to do fishing, singing, dancing, playing games, etc.

Dr. Egan of Sardar Nagar

This is about the summer holidays, when I used to sit idly at home and remain lost in my imaginary world. Sometimes I would go out to play with friends. Then one day I picked up my bicycle and went out to buy books. I was interested in knowing history from the very beginning. On reaching the library, I asked the helper for history books. He gave me various books with colourful covers which were related to the history of India's Mughal period, British rule, and ancient times. There was a brown book on which a picture of an ancient building was drawn, and the title was 'Shaharnama Gorakhpur'. That book attracted me, and I found it hard to resist buying it. As soon as I came home, I started reading about the services and achievements of famous people of my city, in which the first name was Dr. Egan. When I started reading it, I came to know that he was the Hungarian husband of the renowned Indo-Hungarian (cousin)painter Amrita Shergil. He was a famous gynecologist and medical practitioner of Sardar Nagar and had a clinic affiliated to the Saraya Sugar Mills. This information increased my curiosity. Sardar Nagar is near my village, and my grandfather had spent some time there as a veterinarian. I asked him about Dr. Egan, and was told that the locals addressed him as 'Angrezwa Doctor'. He was extremely punctual. It was said that the hospital staff used to match their time with his watch, and he was an intemperate smoker. After getting information from my grandfather, I started searching on the internet, and then I got the contact details of Doctor sahab's daughter, Juliet.

On calling, I introduced myself in English and asked about her father. On asking, her first question was 'How did you get my number and why do you want to know about my father?. I said on the pretext that I want to write an article on her father. After that, she started describing her father. Her father was born on 5th October 1910 in Budapest, Hungary, and completed his education there and came to India after marriage. Juliet tells that she is the younger daughter of Dr Victor Egan. Her elder sister, Eva Sud, now resides in Gurgaon with her family. Their mother was Nina Egan, Dr. Egan's wife after his first wife, Amrita, passed away in 1941. Juliet mentioned that her father had no belief in spiritual beings or God but considered Humanity as his religion. He had his hospital in Sardar Nagar and also had a clinic near the Sher Kothi in Gorakhpur, which was in the city. Whenever he got some time, he used to go to the Railway Club to catch up with his old friends and play a few rounds of cards with them. He enjoyed good food but had no particular preference for any cuisine.

One of the many anecdotes that Juliet mentioned was that once some villagers brought a man to Dr. Egan's hospital, saying he had died and pleading with him to save him. This man had been bitten by a snake, and after removal of the venom and care, the man woke up. The villagers who thought this man had risen from the dead, exclaimed that this was indeed a miracle. To continue with this anecdote, a few poor children, who were being taken care of by the Swedish Mission in nearby Chauri Chaura, were being given classes in Catechism, or the study of God. They were being told stories about Jesus and his miracles. One of them is the story of Jesus resurrecting Lazarus, four days after his burial. All of a sudden, a girl raised her hand and said that she had seen Jesus. He lived in Sardarnagar, and his name was Dr. Egan. This was just one incident depicting the faith that the people had in Dr. Victor Egan. Another very key event is that the famous Bollywood actor Jimmy Shergill, who belongs to the Majithia family, was also born at the hands of Dr. Egan.

He was a very gentle person, in spite of his often getting annoyed at the stupidity of the villagers who would come to him for treatment. He loved and cared for all sorts of birds and animals, and often said his house looked like a zoo. He used to say, 'The more I learn about people, the more I love my dogs, a quote originally said by Mark Twain. This phrase expresses a preference for dogs over humans due to the perceived simplicity and loyalty of dogs compared to the complexity and perceived flaws of humans.

A great human being, a wonderful Doctor, a caring father to his daughters and a trusting and loving husband to his wife (Nina Hydrie) who was 23 years younger to him, this was Dr. Victor Egan, a man who was simple and kind, and who gave up his chances to lead a lavish lifestyle, so that he could live in simplicity, taking care of the people who needed him the most.

Dr. Egan took his last breath in Saraya on the 30th of June 1997. He passed away at the age of 86.

The Potters of Basharatpur

It was the time of the British Raj. Mr. A.G. Potter arrived in India along with his wife. He was posted in the hilly regions of Nainital. Serving as an army veteran in the British army. After getting retired he came to Gorakhpur with his child, Harold. Mr. Harold was enrolled in St. Andrews College. He completed his education from there and then got a job in the Bengal North Western railways as an 'A' grade driver. According to his friends, he was the only one who wore a white uniform and not khaki. His engine was installed with a steel polished handle. He establised his beautiful house, Potters Lodge, in Basharatpur. The house still stands with a beautiful garden and an old European-style bungalow. He married a girl named Elsie Samuel from Basharatpur, and their children were Rodney, Teddy, and Olga. Mr Rodney completed his education from the prestigious La Martiniere and got a job in the Indian Air Force. For his constant services, he was promoted to the post of commandant in the railway protection force. His brother Teddy, who also served in the railways. He was working as a locomotive driver.

Mr. Rodney married Shirley Brendish, and their children are Allen and Pearl.

But unfortunately, Mr. Rodney is no more, and his son Allen lives with his two sons. Allen has also faced the bereavements of his wife, parents, and sister.

The time and situations are different, but the lodge still depicts the joy and blissful days of that time.

The Bayley of Railways

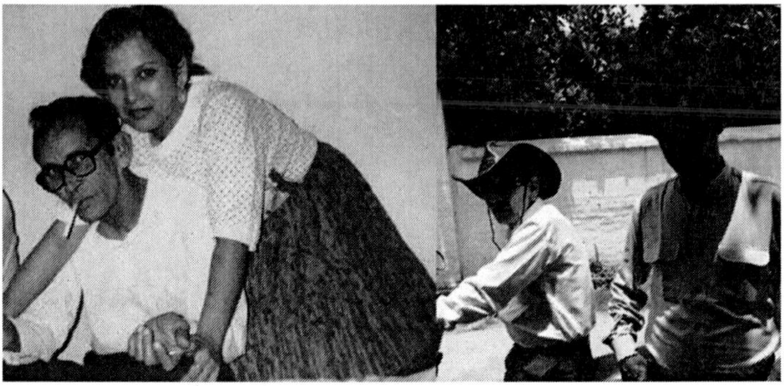

It was evening. I was busy finishing my book. I often contact Mr. Deep Raj Frederick for information. I frequently call him. I asked him for Debra Bayley's contact information.

I called her and introduced myself, saying that I wanted to know about her family. It was a fun conversation that lasted about half an hour. Debra said that her grandfather came to India before independence and worked as a guard in the railways. Her father, Mr. Dennis Bayley, was of Irish-English descent. He worked as an assistant fireman and later became a Grade A driver. During his service, he married Mrs. Maureen Bayley (née D'Cruz), who was of pure European descent. According to Debra, her father received many threats when he went to work during the railway strike, but he did not stop working. Debra completed her schooling at the Railway Mixed Primary

School and received her higher education from Gandhi Girls School in Lucknow. She settled in Gorakhpur in 1971. Her mother, Maureen, worked as a teacher at St. Anthony's School. In Gorakhpur, her family lived in 'Blue Cottage' in Basharatpur. Debra says that she had a very enjoyable childhood because she had six sisters and one brother. Debra says that her father used to organize small house parties where there was singing, dancing, and tambola, and delicious dishes like beef steaks, duck roast, and pork vindaloo were served. Debra shared that her parents were very fond of gardening, which is why they had a small garden. Interestingly, people urged them to open a nursery, which they flatly refused. Debra currently works at an educational institution run started by Mr. Frank Anthony. Debra said that she also had the good fortune of meeting Frank Anthony. One very amusing anecdote shared by Debra is about her maternal grandfather, who was a Sergeant Major in the British Army. And they had also received eight tickets from the British government during the time of independence. Four were for ships and four for airplanes. But the family feared being separated, as tensions were high and there were premonitions of ships sinking and planes crashing. So the family decided to travel together. But that never happened. Debra currently lives in Delhi. She is a retired teacher but still works on an extended basis. Her daughter is married and works as an advocacy advisor in an NGO.

Debra has faced the bereavements of her husband, father, and brother, but leads her life happily, making her an inspiration and ideal for others.

It was a pleasure talking to her.

The Garage Owner - Goddards

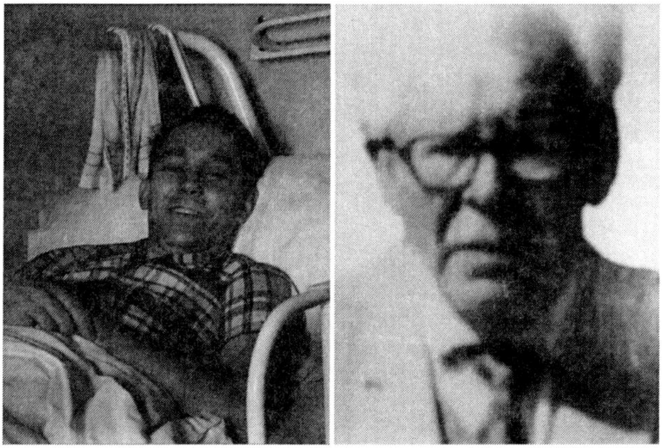

This story starts from the late 1800s when Mr. Vincent Mathias Goddard arrived in India from Ireland along with his wife. Our nation was a British colony at that time. He was sent by the hospitality company to get stationed at the hotel Clarks, Benaras, as an Administrator and Manager. And their child was born in India with Irish parents. So, being in British India, he got his first job as a boatswain officer in the Royal Navy. After leaving his job in the Navy, Mr. Joseph Vincent worked in a cement factory known as Soan Valley Portland situated in Japla, which was a subsidiary of Martin and Burns Co. While serving in his service he got married to Mrs. Teresa Goddard. And one of the children among the four was Brian Joseph, AKA Mukul. Mr. Brian completed his education from Allahabad and then came to Gorakhpur just to manage his father's motor garage business, 'Minnie Automobiles'. This journey commenced in the 1960s. And became one of the most popular garages in the whole city. Even the top doctors like Sohanlal, Dr. Mukherjee, and Dr. Egan were the most trusted clients of this establishment. Not only is this one of the most renowned Aristocrat families, but the Majithias' and Mahant Avaidyanath of Gorakhnath Mandir relied on the services of Minnie Garage.

While talking to Mudit, the son of Mr. Mukul. I got to know that his Irish grandfather was not only fluent in Irish, French, and English but was also very smooth in speaking Hindi, Bhojpuri, Maithili, and Bengali as well.

One of the key anecdotes that Mudit shared was the arrival of an accidental bus from Nepal. There was a foreign couple travelling and exploring the globe in their Volkswagen microbus. But when they reached Nepal, the winding roads and perilous falls led to the accident of their bus. And while searching for a garage, they reached Gorakhpur. And got to know about the 'Minnie'. The task to repair this vehicle was not easy, as it was extremely damaged. But the experience and knowledge of mechanics riveted the parts and got successful in giving a new life to the bus.

The foreign couple travelled the globe without any trouble and reached their motherland successfully. The service was so nice that the garage received a feedback call from the couple.

As the time changes, everyone has to take turns. Now there is no Garage named Minnie on Park Road

The Goddard family has shifted to Lucknow.

Mr Mudit is busy establishing his agricultural business. He lives there with his lovely mother Shirin, father Mukul, and brother Maneet, adoring the Indian culture.

The Rozarios

It was Wednesday that I went to meet Mr. Denzil Lazarus. I was very excited to go there. As I had met Judy mam before, I was worried about the situation. Mr. Lazarus is asleep many times because of his illness. But this time I was lucky as I was having the file with me. I knocked on the gate and waited for a while. Suddenly, I saw a group of dogs running towards the gate.

Going inside was no less than becoming the bait of a hungry lion. Barking of the dogs made Judy mam to open the gate. She pacified the dogs and made me sit on a chair. After waiting for 10 minutes Mr. Denzil came slowly on the support of a stick. I conversed with him for about half an hour and then went to meet Ms. Thelma, who just lives beside their house in a small cottage.

I asked her sister Karen to pen down the history of Rozarios. The family of Crisphin Paul Rozario and Rose Mary Rosario migrated from the East India Company to Calcutta. But later settled in Gorakhpur.

In the late 1800s, it was there that my great-grandfather got a job in the railway as a senior engineer and was allotted the railway quarter named house number 100. They had nine kids: Michael, Ed, Eva, Alice, Dan, William, James, Charles, and Henry. Most of Chrisphin's kids followed in his footsteps by joining the railways. The last person in the family to work for the railways was Ivor Rozario.

James Rosario was married to Daisy Lazarus, and both had four kids- Rodney, Meryn, Daphne, and Ivor. He shifted with his wife, Daisy, to live with his father-in-law. Mr. Ivor was a cleaner for engines in the railways and was later promoted to an 'A' grade driver. The house was famous as 'The Rosario zoo'. Ms. Karen says that her uncle Ivor was a fantastic fisherman. He used to have an imported fishing rod, which he used to take during picnics to catch fish in the Kushmi Jungle and Naanpara.

The most interesting anecdote that Ms Karen enunciatedwas the story of her grandfather, a snakebite curer. Usually, villagers used to come from Chauri Chaura, Maharajganj, Peppeganj to get their family members treated by her grandfather. Once, a 12-year-old son of a sarpanch came to him, bleeding, with him to save his son, who was bitten by three snakes. The situation was critical as the venom had infected the whole body. But the experience of Mr. James Morgen saved him. It took three days to inoculate the venom.

According to Karen, Christmas was the most important day. A beautiful occasion where the families dressed elegantly and visited the church. The night was meant for parties.

This was the fun and frolic childhood of Karen. Frequently resides in Pune with her two kids. It was a pleasure talking and discussing the forgotten past of the Anglo Indian community.

The Lazarus family of Mohaddipur

In the same series is Mr. Denzil Lazarus, who lives in Mohaddipur.

Mr. Lazarus was the first leader of the Anglo Indian community of Gorakhpur and was a part of the Indian National Congress.

His grandfather, James Morgan Lazarus, was the first to come to Gorakhpur in the late 1800s. He was posted here as a sanitary inspector. After retirement, he purchased a land from Miyan Sahib in the notified area (now Mohaddipur) and established a beautiful house, which is now more than 100 years old.

His son was Stanley Joseph Lazarus.

Stanley too worked for the North Eastern railways as a Loco inspector. His wife was Kathleen Disney.

Their child, Denzil was born on the 10th October, 1942.

Mr. Denzil was enrolled in St. Andrews Intermediate College for his primary education. After passing out from St. Andrews, He was put to Mahatma Gandhi Inter College for further studies. Mr. Lazarus worked as a goods supplier to Nepal. He was married to Ms. Judy Ledlie of Anand Nagar, whose father, Dorcas Iris Ledlie, was a medical officer in the government hospital. Mrs.

Judy tells that during the Raj, her grandparents were the jailors of the Kanpur Jail, both male and female sections respectively.

Mr. Denzil enunciates that his father was a fantastic violinist and every party used to be held at the terrace of his residence.

One of the interesting parts in this talk was that he used to travel to Nepal on his motorbike, accompanied by his wife and son.

In his childhood, he used to visit kushmi jungle and the Domingarh lake on his bicycle. He had a fun and frolic childhood.

Mr. Denzil's son is Neville. He is a journalist for Sky News and has covered some of the top incidents, like the war in the Gulf of Afghanistan and the Delhi CAA NRC protest. He is known for reporting in the most vulnerable situations.

Mr. Neville has won several awards, also, two of them being the BAFTA and an EMMY.

Mr. Denzil and his wife are leading a happy retired life with the seven other members of their family, their beautiful dogs.

The Savaille family

It was a very difficult task for me to contact the Anglo Indians who are living on every corner of our city.

While searching, I met the Savaille family.

Mr. Edwin Savaille lives in the Shrirampuram colony. He is a retired railway employee. He lives with his wife, Shahjahan Savaille.

Mrs. Savaille was a teacher in H.P Children's Academy, Sahara Estate. Mr. Edwin's sister now lives in New Zealand.

Their father, Wifred Douglas Savaille, was an Assistant Workshop Manager in the railways, and their mother was a teacher in St Anthony.

They lived in the bungalow located in the Dairy colony, Asuran. Mr. Edwin's son works at American Express.

His daughter Sharon is married in Dublin, and Serena works in a Corporate company situated in the NCR region.

Railway Mix Primary School

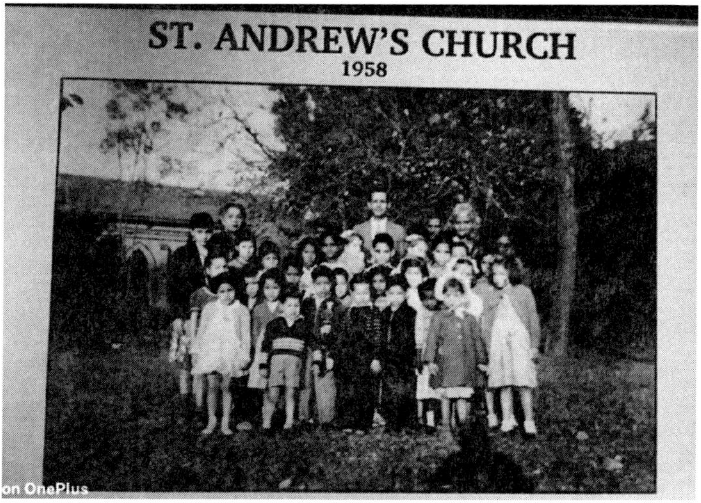

EUGENE IS AN AMAZING person; he knows just about everything there is to know about life in railway colonies in pre-partition India. And his knowledge has not been gained secondhand through research. Eugene has lived all through his boyhood in railway colonies here in Central India, where his father worked for the Bengal

Nagpur Railway. And he has great tales to tell about life in these colonies. He explored the backyards of nearly every home in his neighbourhood when he was a boy. And the fragrance of these homes still lingers on him, as fresh as ever. His work in Britain's RAF has not dulled his longing for a whiff of the good old times back home in India.

Eugene's knowledge is phenomenal; he has enlightened me with many fascinating tales from his boyhood days. And he tells me that since earliest times, every railway colony in the country had a church in it, most often the Church of England, but sometimes Roman Catholic. This was a startling revelation for me. Back in the early seventies, my father was posted in Gorakhpur, where we attended St Andrew's Church, a magnificent brick edifice, set amidst the sprawling railway colony. I was but a lad of twelve then, winding my way through the streets of the colony, my mind often wondered how a church came to be in the midst of these brick red homes. The answer was to come only several years later. The topmost cadres in the railway administration in those times were occupied by Britishers, while routine jobs and operating posts were held by Anglo Indians, fiercely proud of their association with the railways of India. To ensure all-round growth and a well-balanced personality among its workforce, the railways provided each of its colonies with an institute for recreation, an English medium school for the children staying in the colony, parks, officers' clubs, and a church. The colony was thus self-sufficient in itself, a small township whose inhabitants were well-provided for in all respects, not needing to look elsewhere for any of their needs, not even for a place of worship.

And so here I was, a boy of twelve, whistling a tune to myself as I trudged along to attend the railway school, satchel slung around my shoulder. Built in true railway style, the school was an architectural marvel in brickwork with a large playground at the back, and a large lunch hall furnished with benches and water taps where we tiny-tots gathered in the afternoon with our tiffin boxes. Next to the school building was the railway institute, tall and graceful, standing amidst majestic silence, the wind playing on its twin towers in a soft caress, while an occasional hoot of an engine followed by a rattle of wheels reminded me that a train was making its way out of the railway yard nearby. Oh, for a taste of those days again! The railway primary school I attended was staffed by ladies, many of whom lived in the railway colony itself. And quite a few of these dear aunties were Christians who attended church. There was Mrs Newbolt, the Headmistress, fair, tall, and aloof. Then there was Miss Clifford, who taught us Social Studies, Mrs Joseph, Mrs Cecil, and others, many of them familiar to us as members of St Andrew's Church. Each Sunday, the crisp morning air of the colony echoed with the toll of the bell high up on the steeple. Jangle-jangle chimed the bell, while families dressed in Sunday best would be seen walking up the driveway for morning worship. Many a young lad like me stood watching spellbound as Musa, the sexton, tugged at the cable that hung down, causing the huge bell atop the church to swing, giving out a rhythmic musical peal.

The bell atop St Andrew's is tolled twice each week, once for morning service and the other for evensong. Morning service was always more formal and was attended by the cream of the congregation. There were the Browns and Benjamins and their sons, the Josephs, Cecils, and Amarnaths. After-church gatherings in the church premises were tinged with a butterfly touch when the men gathered in small groups, lost in profound conversation, while the womenfolk flitted about speaking in low whispers, letting out occasional giggles. Some folks like the Chandis kept out of the general talk; they preferred to keep aloof, standing quietly beside their car. The seven years we lived in this town in eastern U.P. saw a succession of parsons who held charge over St Andrew's, beginning with the quiet Pastor Lall, followed by Rev Baldeo, Pitamber, and others. Week after week, these men watched over their flock, expounding the

Word for all, exhorting men to turn back from the world and its ways and follow the path of honesty and godliness. Occasionally, a guest speaker would be called in to preach. I can still remember the clear tones of the Reverend William Paul, an English missionary, speaking out from the pulpit on one occasion. Lean, tall, and fair, Reverend Paul was a much-loved figure in Gorakhpur. He lived in an old-style bungalow in Basaratpur, and we had the pleasure of having him in our home a few times, accompanied by his Canadian wife.

Having stayed in India for years, Paul finally had to prepare to return to England. We went to see him in Basaratpur and found his wife had laid out several articles on a table to be given away to friends for a small price. Mother bought some cutlery and several cut glass bowls. Then there was an old Viewmaster with several reels that we took home with us.

There was hardly a crowd beside the first class carriage at the station when we went to see off the gentleman and his wife. My hand was in a cast after a fall, and I was subdued, though inwardly excited to be at the station. The whistle blew, but Paul was unperturbed. He nimbly walked up to me and, holding the cast in his hand, signed his name on it. W. M. Paul. This was his parting gift to me. It was something anyone would treasure. Then, as the night express to Allahabad jerked forward, Paul smartly moved, and with one bound, he was aboard, waving us goodbye as the train slowly pulled out.

But it was Evensong at St Andrew's we liked to attend, for it was held in the cool of the day, and was more a relaxed affair free from the formalism of the morning service. Thus, each Sunday evening found us preparing for a ride through the railway colony. For a fare of only Re 1, the rickety old rickshaw would take us past the railway sports stadium, go right over the level crossing of Mohaddipur, and then into the depths of the colony lined with tamarind trees. It was incredibly calm here. As the rickshaw creaked on, all you could hear was the rustle of the branches overhead, the distant cries of children playing, and the occasional rumble of a train. We rode past railwaymen's bungalows, neat and clean, set amidst an overgrowth of neem and mango trees. We ride on through Private Road, bypass the turning that leads to my school, and cross a square. The rickshaw grinds to a halt beside a gate, and we alight. St Andrew's is now in full view, thrusting its spire into the crimson sky and bathed in the soft light of the setting sun.

The place is aglow with life in the evenings: bees and insects swarm through the air, settling on hedges of pansies and snapdragons, while birds of all descriptions congregate on trees, chirping excitedly, preparing for the night's rest ahead. St Andrew's church was truly set in paradise.

Evensong was held by the Reverend Caleb Bellah, a short, stout, cheery old man, as cheerful and vivacious as the birds now settling in the trees around. Bellah was, in fact, a pastor employed with a Christian girls' orphanage, but as a sideline to his work, he often volunteered to undertake the evening service at St Andrew's. He was a man given to brevity; he believed that a church service should be short enough to be effective, and to this end, he would order the evening's proceedings so as never to last for more than an hour. His sermons were always a pleasure to sit through; they were well-planned and thought out, and although he read his text aloud from a typed sheet, he would give away cyclostyled copies which we were allowed to carry home. With never more than about a dozen persons in attendance, Evensong was a truly enriching experience, quite like an informal prayer gathering in the home.

The final hymn was sung, and the benediction said, we emerged from church. It was dark by now as the little group stood chatting beside the magnificent edifice built in brick. It was a quiet little group; often there would be none besides my father, mom, my sister, the pastor, and his daughter and son-in-law. Then, under the dim street lamps of Private Road, we would begin our trek home with Pastor Bellah by our side, his vigour undiminished by the labours of the evening. And on we walked, sharing our tales of joy and sorrow with the old man, while the bungalows on either side, now alight, seemed to peek at us through rows of hedges and foliage. We walk on under the canopy of trees until we reach the railway. Here we slacken our pace, for we have often to wait till a shunting train has moved out of the way and backed into the yard from whence it came. Beyond the yard is a busy thoroughfare, and here we come to a halt waiting for a rickshaw to appear, which will carry us back home before bidding goodnight to the cheery old parson.

The church of St Andrew still stands, a lone sentinel pointing the way to heaven amidst the jungle of trees and shrubs of Gorakhpur's railway colony. Today, a new group of worshippers may be seen in the pews on Sunday. New faces have appeared, new voices, a different gathering. The old congregation we had known is not to be seen anymore. After a space of four decades, many of its veteran leaders and elders have gone on to be with the Lord; the children who graced the flowering gardens with their colourful attire and cries of play are now grown-ups who have moved away to distant lands in search of greener pastures. But the church itself remains unchanged, as of old. The bell atop the steeple still rings the same chime, calling forth souls to praise and worship. And the story it has to tell is the same old story, a tale of glad tidings for all.

In continuation of this, Ms. PC Clifford pen downs some amazing stories of the railway School when she was working there as a teacher. On the insistence of my mother, I joined the railway School in the year 1960. At that time, Ms.

M.A Williams and Mrs. Howard were there.One of my dear colleagues, Mrs. P.L Herbert, was contemporary to me and later became the head of the primary section. Ms. Meera Mukherjee was the music teacher. It was in the midst of the railway colony. Being an English medium school, it was considered the finest institution in the city, particularly meant for the children of the railway officials. Later on, the kids of Air force personnels also joined the school.Our school principal, Mrs. I.J Newbolt, was very disciplined, and so was the environment of our school. In the beginning majority of the students were Anglo Indians, their names being Jennifer Wadley, Adrian Carter, Moira Willis, Pearl Potter, and Debra Bayley .

Many Anglo Indian students were later put into the Oakgrove School, which is a 103-year-old institution meant for the railway people.

All the officers' bungalows had a servant quarter adjacent to the building. So, the kids of the clerks and peons used to attend the school. But, there was no discrimination among the students. Many of the children did really well and are now doctors and professors in some of the top institutions

Macedo's Bakery

Macedo's Bakery in Gorakhpur occupies a unique place in the social and cultural memory of the city. In earlier decades, it was not only a favored destination for politicians, sports personalities, and scholars, but also a popular meeting place for young couples. The bakery became widely known for its freshly baked buns, rich butter, aromatic coffee, and a variety of patties and cakes that attracted visitors from across the region.

This story dates back to the period of British rule in India, when a Goan Christian, Aouino Thomas Macedo, constructed a residence along Geeta Vatika Road and established a restaurant named Savariya. Founded in 1942, the eatery quickly earned a reputation for its distinctive butter and buns. Much like Hazratganj in Lucknow, Civil Lines in Allahabad, Connaught Place in Delhi, and the famous coffee houses of Patna that served as intellectual and political gathering spaces, Savariya too emerged as an important meeting point in Gorakhpur's public life.

In later years, Aouino Macedo's son, Emile John Macedo, transformed the restaurant into a confectionery and renamed it Macedo Bakery. Over time, the establishment grew beyond a simple bakery and evolved into a central hub of political discussion in the Purvanchal region. Influential leaders and emerging political figures frequently gathered here, using the informal setting to exchange ideas and shape strategies. Leaders such as Veer Bahadur Singh, Kalpnath Rai, student leader-turned-MLA Ravindra Singh, and Rajnath Singh were among those who were associated with the bakery during its most active years.

As years passed, the name and form of the establishment changed, and it came to be known simply as Macedos. Around 1982, when Emile Macedo decided to relocate to Canada, he chose to sell the bakery. Although several offers were made, he ultimately handed it over to the building's owner, Kalimul Haq. Before leaving, Macedo received a promise that both the name and the distinctive taste of the bakery would be preserved.

The bakery continued to attract a wide range of visitors. Veer Bahadur Singh was known to frequent nearby shops but remained fond of the bakery's tea and cutlets. Renowned badminton player Syed Mehdi Rizvi Modi was also a regular visitor, often accompanied by Amita Kulkarni, who later became the Maharani of Amethi. Playback singer Daler Mehndi, during his early years in Gorakhpur while learning music under Rahat Ali in Jatepur, was likewise drawn to Macedos and continues to recall those memories fondly. Mr. Callender, a resident of Basharatpur, was another frequent patron, and many railway employees made the bakery their regular evening meeting place for conversation and relaxation.

Although everyday citizens may gradually forget the journey of Macedos, those who rose to prominence—whether in politics or other fields—continue to remember its importance. Much like the iconic coffee houses of Delhi, Allahabad, Lucknow, and Patna, Macedos held a special status in Gorakhpur. In many ways, it influenced the direction of regional politics in Purvanchal. The legacy of the bakery still lingers in the city, carried forward through memories and stories.

Macedos once occupied a vital position in the political circles of eastern Uttar Pradesh, where critical decisions and alliances were often discussed. From Veer Bahadur Singh's early political rise to Virendra Pratap Shahi's transition from crime to public life, many pivotal moments were shaped within the modest hall of this historic establishment

Citation - "Shaharnama Gorakhpur" by Dr. Ved Prakash Pandey

THE GOSPEL

Geography of Basharatpur

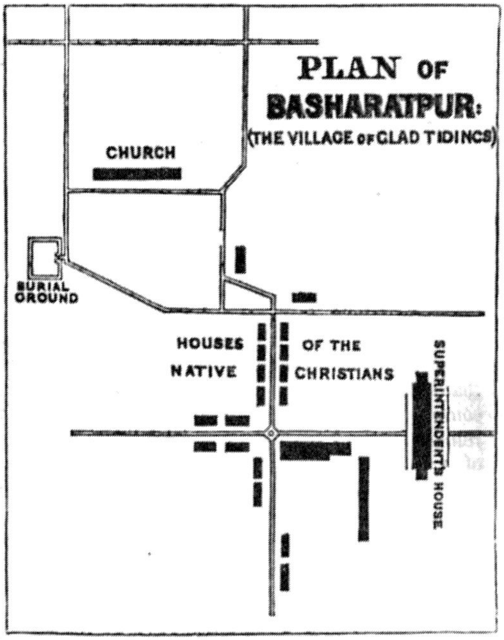

It was hard to find the exact scenario of the Village but I have collected some information through personal interviews. Basharatpur was a village extending in 1500 acres. The south of St. John's Church is Chargawan and

Pipraich Road. To the North is Dharampur, Sudhi Bagia (Moti Pokhara) and Asuran Chungi. To the south west is pachpedwa and Fertilizer Colony.

The yellow house (now of Mr. Rajesh Singh), in front of the Church gate, was the parsonage of C.M.S where Ms. Dilis Morgan and Mrs. Oliver used to live.

Adjacent to it was the boys' orphanage.

On the street of Ashok Nagar is Mahima Kuti, which was the parsonage of the Zenana mission where Ms. Traina and Ms. Ventura resided.

Then talking about the green-colored house adjacent to the church gate was in the care of the Banerjee family, and the Kothi at the beginning of Dharampur colony was the Stern Kothi, where Rev. Henry Stern resided. Now going to the West Zone is the parsonage of Rev. Sanjay Vincent, where a widow's home was attached adjacent to the mission bungalow. Aam Bazar had a parsonage of Cathechist In Charge, Cornelius, which later taken care by the Rawson Family.

The Mission School still stands at the Tiraha, which extends to the East. The school was in the charge of Mr. J Greenfield.

Rev. Wybrow Frederick died of Malaria because of living near the church tank.

Going straight to the water tank road is the Farriers Park, where Mr. JH Farrier, the manager of the CMS mission compound, used to have evening strolls.

The majority of the mission property is now in the care of the LDTA, Mr. Morris Clement being the property officer..

Sternpur

Located in the northern part of the city, Sternpur has a unique history dating back to 1828. Before 1850, Rev. Henry Stern, who came from England, established this village in the shape of a Holy Cross. At that time, the area was sparsely populated and inhabited by illiterate and unemployed people. To instill a love of learning in them, a hut was built in 1828, and the work of educating these people began. Gradually, people were also introduced to faith alongside education. This faith eventually manifested itself in the form of a large church, which was named St. Mark's Church.

Gorakhpur's St. Mark Church has been spreading the light of education since then.

Around 1825, the priest cleared the forest and settled Sternpur, naming it after himself. He built a hut made of mud bricks for his people and worshipped Jesus Christ there for many years.

Children also received education there. As a result, several generations from this area are now working in good jobs in various places. The people who left this place did not forget their roots and contributed to the development of Sternpur along with their own progress.

Padri Bazaar was established by Rev. Henry Stern on January 27, 1916. The market was in the middle of the city, and it was the priest's wish that all the necessary goods for the people be available in the market. They also wanted to make local goods available in the market.

Therefore, they invited traders from all around and established a market. The market, known as Padri Bazaar, has been operating ever since and continues to this day. It has been more than 100 years since the market was established. Ajit Lawrence explained that during Father Stern's tenure, there was a St. Mark's Parish School in the church premises. People from the surrounding area came here for education and religious instruction. To integrate education with worship, Rev. Henry Stern established a small place of worship in a hut.

His aim in establishing this place of worship was to encourage people to stay away from social evils and vices, and to move towards a civilized society by combining education with faith. And that is exactly what happened. He said that today, several generations later, people from this area are working in various prestigious institutions, bringing honor to Rev. Henry Stern's name. A large number of people worship Lord Jesus Christ in the church.

Christ Church

Christ Church is located at the Shastri Chowk.

It was established in the year 1820 by the then Collector R.M Bird.

He collected donations for the erection of this beautiful monument. The hall has a seating capacity of 200 people, looks majestic with thick, 22-foot-high pillars standing on each side.

15- foot-high wooden doors on each side, the pews, and pictures of Jesus Christ, including a rare Belgian -made glass painting showing Christ carrying children in his arms, add to the beauty of the well-ventilated Church. The central cylindrical-shaped dome with a large cross atop it and a portico attracts visitors.

Also, there used to be a big British-era mechanical clock fitted on the front of the dome, which later became dysfunctional and was replaced with a portrait of Christ. The Belgian glass on which the portrait is painted was gifted by the Campiers.

The two-acre campus with greenery all around and flowering plants makes the Church campus vibrant. The marble plaque inside the Church has an illustration of RM Bird, who established it between 1820 and 1830, and Daniel Wilson, Bishop of Calcutta and metropolitan of India, who consecrated it on March 1, 1841. The plaque describes the theme of the church as 'The rich and poor meet together. The Lord is the maker of them all.'

St. Andrews Church

St. Andrews church was established by the Bengal North Western Railway Company to fulfill the prayer needs of fellow Europeans and Anglo Indians.

The church was consecrated on the 11th of September, 1898 by the then Bishop Rev. Clifford. The first pastor ordained was Thomas Underwood, who used to travel on his green fat bicycle.

St. John's Church

St. John's Church: From a **"Hut of Mud & Straw"** to **"Church in the Wilderness"** and at last the Glorious:- **"St. John's Church"**, Basharatpur (Present Structure)

St. John's Church was established in 1835 in a hut by Rev. Michael Wilkinson. A small congregation of Basharatpur used to attend this church. Later this hut church was vandalized and demolished in the mutiny. After this atrocity a new church building was raised which was extended with two new wings on the either sides. In the year 2000 the church was renovated with the help of the congregation. A stone was installed on the completion of its 200 years. Dr. Paul Dhinakaran being the chief guest.

S.NO	NAMES	TENURE
1	REV. MICHAEL WILKINSON	1823 - 1830
2	REV. W. SMITH	1830 - 1831
3	REV. MICHAEL WILKINSON	1831 - 1839
4	REV. FREDRICK WYBROW	1840
5	REV. F. A. KREISS	1840
6	REV. J. P. MENGE	1840 - 1843
7	REV. J. C. WENDNAGEL	1843 - 1846
8	REV. A. ACHESON	1847 - 1849
9	MR. DERAVERA	1849 - 1853
10	REV. HENRY STERN	1853 - 1894
11	REV. ISSAC VINCENT	1894 - 1896
12	REV. JOHN QALANDER	1897 - 1901
13	REV. W. J. RICHARDS	1919 - 1921
14	REV. Y. DHARAMJIT	1921 - 1930
15	REV. B. PETER	1930 - 1932
16	REV. W. J. RICHARDS	1932 - 1938
17	REV. L. D. DANIEL	1938 - 1941
18	REV. JACOB R. RAFI	1941 - 1943
19	REV. C. RAWSON	1943 - 1947
20	REV. JACOB R. RAFI	1947 - 1948
21	REV. W. J. RICHARDS	1948 - 1949
22	REV. JULIOUS MARTIN REID	1949 - 1950
23	REV. D. A. SAMPSON	1950 - 1953
24	REV. J. S. THAKORE	1953 - 1955
25	REV. J. G. PRAKASH	1955 - 1956
26	REV. I. U. HAQQ	1956 - 1958
27	REV. MARQUS JASWANT	1958 - 1961
28	REV. S. U. MASIH	1961 - 1967
29	REV. P. B. SANTRAM	1967 - 1968
30	REV. FR. JOHN LUKA LALL	1968 - 1970
31	REV. YUSUF ANDRIYAS	1970 - 1977
32	REV. JAMES SAADAT ULLAH	1977 - 1980
33	REV. GEORGE SOLOMON	1980 - 1986
34	REV. SIMON P. SINGH	1986 - 1987
35	REV. JOHN S. WALLACE	1987 - 2001
36	REV. GABRIAL DAUD	2001 - 2002
37	REV. SANJAY VINCENT	2002 - 2019
38	REV. ROSHAN LAL	2019 -

St. Martin Church

St. Martin Church was established in 1937.

It was established on a private subscription and was erected by the family of Mr. Patrick Lyall, who used to live just behind the church.

It was known as Lal Girja due to its red brickwork, but the structure was put down by the administration due to road construction.

A new church building was raised in 2021 and was consecrated on the 14th of November by the then Bishop Rev. Peter Baldev.

St. Joseph's Church

St. Joseph's Church is catholic. It was established in the year 1860 to fulfill the worship needs of the military officers. Bishop Hartmann's records indicate that around 1835, there were a few Catholic soldiers and Christian families here, whose spiritual upkeep was occasionally attended by a priest from Bettiah. The name of any particular priest or the number of Catholic families is not mentioned. It appears that laborers for indigo cultivation came from outside in the early nineteenth century. The Reverend Father Livorni, the first Catholic priest appointed to Gorakhpur in 1860, built St. Joseph's Church in Civil Lines. The first and last entries recorded between July

18, 1860, and October 23, 1862, indicate 27 sacraments of baptism, 19 sacraments of confirmation, 5 marriages, and 18 deaths. Other church records indicate that 325 Catholic soldiers were in the cantonment, and some other Catholics engaged in indigo cultivation lived in the town. Gorakhpur, which later became a part of the Diocese of Agra, was attached to the Diocese of Allahabad in 1886.

In 1892, an Irish priest, Reverend Father Joseph Hickey, came to Gorakhpur and carried out some missionary work. In 1885, Gorakhpur was connected to the rest of the country by rail. Many local and expatriate Catholics arrived by rail. This increased the number of Catholic Christians in Gorakhpur. Over time, it became the headquarters of several mission institutions. In 1906, priests from Gorakhpur also visited neighboring districts.

The Reverend Father T. Consodine lived here for 25 years. Meanwhile, the Catholic population grew. With the appointment of Father Francis Pillai in 1936, Gorakhpur became a major center of many activities.

In 1946, Gorakhpur was separated from the Allahabad Diocese, establishing the Gorakhpur-Varanasi Prefecture Apostolic, which was later entrusted to the Capuchin priests.

Orebro Mission (Sweden)

The Örebro Mission was a Protestant Christian movement that originated in Sweden. It was established in the town of Örebro in 1892 by Baptist pastor John Ongman and initially functioned under the Baptist Union of Sweden until 1936. Much later, in 1997, the mission became part of the Evangelical Free Church in Sweden.

The work of the Örebro Mission extended beyond Europe and eventually reached India. Its activities first entered the Gorakhpur district and later expanded into the regions of Bengal. Evangelist Clas Emil Sjögren was appointed to serve as a missionary among the Indian population. Acting on his own initiative, Sjögren traveled to England, where he spent six months at Livingstone College receiving basic medical training along with instruction in languages. At that time, the mission organization did not operate any overseas missions. Nevertheless, with the encouragement and support of Pastor John Ongman, Sjögren was commissioned and sent to India in the autumn of 1908 by the Baptist congregation known as Philadelphia in Örebro.

During his stay in India, Sjögren's health deteriorated severely, and he contracted tuberculosis. In response, the congregation decided to send additional support in the form of Lydia Magnusson, who had previously worked with the Alliance Mission in India and was already familiar with the Hindi language, along with Helga Modig, a trained midwife who later became known as Helga Hammarsten. Both women had been inspired to pursue missionary service through the influence of Fredrik Franson. They traveled by ship to Bombay and then continued onward to Gorakhpur. Upon arriving in the autumn of 1910, they learned that Sjögren had passed away only a few weeks earlier.

Following this unexpected loss, the two women resolved to establish their own area of mission work. They were advised by Miss Adams, an Indian Bible scholar and associate of the well-known revivalist Pandita Ramabai, to focus on the United Provinces of northern India, later known as Uttar Pradesh. In this region, located along the plains of the Ganges, missionaries from the Church Missionary Society were already active in Gorakhpur. These missionaries directed the Swedish workers toward the several tahsils around the district.

Missionary activity formally began in April 1911 in the town of Barhaj under the name Swedish Baptist Mission in North India. In 1917, this work was officially taken over by the Örebro Mission. Over time, the mission expanded into several nearby locations. The region was primarily agrarian and formed an important cultural and religious center, characterized by a strong Hindu presence alongside a significant Muslim population. The historically important site of Kushinagar, traditionally believed to be the place where Gautama Buddha attained parinirvana, is situated close to this area.

By the end of 1911, additional missionaries arrived, including Frank Henriksson, followed by others in subsequent years. The first recorded baptism of an Indian believer did not take place until 1913. This individual was Hira Firangi, a man from a marginalized caste, who, after interaction with Henriksson, expressed his desire to follow the teachings of Jesus. During the first twenty-five years of mission activity, six small congregations were established. By 1935, their combined membership stood at only 333 individuals.

In 1933, a revival movement emerged within these congregations, beginning in Deoria. This renewal brought greater spiritual depth and organizational stability to the churches. Gradually, the number of believers increased, and by the closing years of the twentieth century, membership had grown to approximately 2,000.

Barhaj

Mr. Frank Henricksson landed at Barhaj in November 1911. All the believers met together to worship God and praise Him for the opportunity to present the gospel in an area where no Missionary or Preacher had ever been before.

The small group of Missionaries, Preachers, and Bible Women, about 10 persons, established the first Church of this Mission at Barhaj on Easter Sunday, 1912 (7th April 1912).

In the same year, a deadly in nature, Plague, broke out around Barhaj. It didn't spare anybody in the vicinity where the infection had reached the rats. Family after family was wiped out within a few days, and those who were healthy left their houses leaving their relatives unattended, who were victimised by the plague. But these missionaries used to visit these patients.

During a visit, they met a person whom they had already met off and on, who was a victim of Plague. The village was quite deserted; even his wife was not there. These Missionaries knelt and prayed for his healing. They continued visiting him, nursing him till he was completely cured. After a few days, he walked to the Mission compound to give thanks to the Missionaries for their prayer and support when everybody had forsaken him. Day by day, his visits to the Mission compound increased, and he was taught about the love of Jesus Christ and that salvation is only through Him. The day came when he took baptism in the river Ghaghra on 22nd January 1913. He was the first non-Christian who got converted to Christianity in this area. His name was Firangi (father of Pastor Emanuel Gunnar). Later on, his wife took baptism after two years. By & by, other relatives and other non-Christians accepted the Lord Jesus Christ as their personal Saviour and joined the Church after taking water baptism.

During the First World War (28th September 1914-11th November 2018), the flow of the Missionaries from Sweden stopped. But the then Missionaries opened an orphanage for poor boys and girls roaming about in search of food and clothes. In the beginning, there were 198 boys and girls. Quite a good number of them ran away when the situation became normal, but some remained at Barhaj. Later on, the girls were sent to Deoria, and the boys stayed at Barhaj. It is remarkable to note that some of them became preachers in our field.

Primary Boarding School was opened in 1928, and it became a Junior High School in 1958.

Barhalganj

The next Missionary who came to India was Mr. Karl Hammersten, who arrived at Barhaj in December 1913 and moved to Barhalganj, the outpost of Barhaj. In November 1917, he married Miss Helga Modig, who was working at Deoria; he did not live long because of the Asian Flu and died on 9th December 1918.

The evangelistic work was carried on at Barhalganj by the Missionaries and evangelists from Barhaj, especially during winter. It was very difficult to obtain suitable housing accommodation for Missionaries at Barhalganj. During cold weather, the Missionaries and Evangelists lived in a tent and engaged in spreading the Gospel of salvation and also in securing suitable land on which the Mission House was to be erected. It was not until 1921 that Missionaries settled down here in a rented house in the market with the intention to open a third Mission Station, after Barhaj and Deoria. On 1st April 1923, a Church was organized with 11 persons. The Mission bungalow was dedicated in October of the same year. The necessary buildings for Mission workers have been erected in the Mission compound in due course of time. The Church building was erected in 1940. Besides, two outstations- Gola and Bans Gaon were opened. At Gola, a primary school was opened. Evangelistic work was being carried on these stations.

The first three persons, who accepted Lord Jesus Christ as their savior, were Ganpat, Sampat, and Jaikari; some of their offspring are in Gorakhpur at present.

In 1950, Miss. L Oberge, an evangelist, and Miss. A. Linderberg, a fully trained Nurse came to Barhalganj. Miss. Oberge used to go outside for preaching work and Miss. Linderberg started a small dispensary at the verandah of Mission Bungalow. Later on, in 1964-65, a piece of land was bought adjacent to the existing Mission Compound and the present Seva Sadan Christian The hospital building was erected in 1966. As long as Miss. Linderberg was at Barhalganj, the Hospital was growing well and doing charity work as there was no lack of foreign funds, but as she retired and went back to Sweden, the foreign funds stopped, and work was hampered a lot.

Deoria

In the beginning, our Mission work was confined to Barhaj only. But as the new Missionaries came out, the question of starting Mission work at another place in the district became acute. In September 1912, the following article appeared in our Mission paper: "Dear Mission Friends and Co-workers. As you know, we expect to welcome two new Missionaries this fall, and as there is no housing accommodation available for more than two Missionaries here at Barhaj, we intend to open a new Mission station. We have been praying to God that He should guide us in the choice of a new place in this district, where we may be able to establish a new Mission station. We have been guided by God to go to Deoria, a city between Barhaj and Gorakhpur. In anticipation of the arrival of the new Missionaries, we have been able to obtain a house there.

We intend to start work there on October 1st". From this record, we find that the work was started on 1 October 1912 at Deoria.

The third Missionary who came to India was Mr. Frank Henricksson, who landed at Barhaj in November 1911. With the influx of the Missionaries, they felt that there was no need for all of them to live in one place, so the ladies Missionaries (Lydia Magnusson and Helga Modig) left Barhaj and went to Deoria. When they came to Deoria, there was no Mission station to live in. On account of the extreme housing shortage in the city at that time, no adequate house suitable for Missionaries was available. But the first Missionaries in a new field were compelled to bear temporary inconvenience; a small house was used for some time as the residence of Missionaries. In December 1912, the fourth Missionary, Miss Hanna Bjogvist, came to India and joined other ladies at Deoria in a rented house. Later on, in November 1915, she married Mr.

Frank Henricksson and moved to Barhaj, where they lived till their retirement. People called them 'Papa ji' and'Mama ji' because of their popularity. There seems to have been greater interest among our Mission friends in the homeland for Deoria than for Barhaj, because already in 1913 a Mission bungalow and quarters for the Indian workers were erected at Deoria, while Barhaj had to wait until 1917 for its bungalow. At an early date, a Church was organized at Deoria. But unfortunately, no record has been preserved regarding the time when this Church was organized. It is recorded that there were in 1918, 40 members in this Church. For many years, there was no Church building at Deoria. All services were held in the verandah of the Mission bungalow.

Almost at the very beginning, the orphanage for girls opened at Barhaj, shifted to Deoria, which was later on moved to Chauri Chaura in 1924. The earlier Missionaries felt the need of young people to learn a trade and thus earn their livelihood. They sent some to different Missions for professional training. But after some time, the Missionaries started a Carpentry School in Deoria. They also felt the need for trained Evangelists in our Mission, and hence they used to send them to other Theological Institutes. As the need became more acute, Rev. & Mrs. F. B. Rehnstrom, who came to Deoria in 1920, started a Theological School there in 1930. There were not many students in the beginning. To enshrine the memory of two great pioneer leaders of Orebro Mission, Rev. Ongman and Rev. Karlsson, a Church was erected in 1932, named 'Ongman - Karlsson Memorial Church'. All the expenses were paid by the Missionaries and Indian Christians from our Churches. After the great revival in Deoria Church in 1933, which spread to all our Mission Stations, several young boys of the Carpentry School willingly left the Carpentry trade and joined the Theological School. Some names of the students who also served this Mission are Mr. Jhapti Dutt, Mr. Hira Lal, Mr. Emmanuel Das, Mr. Nar Singh, Mr. Sukat Benzamine, Mr. Prem Masih, etc.The Theological School was shifted to Gorakhpur when Rev. & Mrs. F. B. Rehnstrom started a new Mission Station in 1937. Mr. Emmanuel Gunnar was a student of the last batch of this Theological School in the year 1942.

In the year 2024, the Church Committee decided to expand the Church building by the extension of one of its wings. So on 19-04-2024 foundation stone was laid down for this work, and on

13-11-2025, the extended portion was inaugurated. The Missionaries/ Pastors who serve this Church are-

Missionaries-

Miss. Lydia Magnusson, Miss Helga Modig, Miss Hanna Sjogvist, Rev. & Mrs. F. B. Rehenstrom, Rev. & Mrs. Edwardsson, Rev. & Mrs. Evert Eriksson, Rev. & Mrs. Nelson.

Pastors-

Pastor Lachchan Lal, Pastor D. S. Khan, Pastor James John, Pastor Emmanuel Das, Pastor J. Frankey, Pastor R.S. Basumata, Pastor Rakesh John, Pastor S. Isaiah, Pastor N. Suman, and presently Pastor Nitin Robert.

Chauri Chaura

Chauri Chaura had been an outstation of Deoria for years. In 1922, Miss. Signe Eklof and Miss E. Hjelmberg

came to Deoria. They were assigned to take care of the orphanage for girls. Later on, in 1924, they moved to Chauri Chaura. Mr. Prem Das went to Chauri Chaura to work with these two missionaries. There, they got a piece of infertile sandy land from the landlord Sardar ji of Sardar Nagar. A Mission bungalow, Preacher's quarter, and hostel for girls were erected. A Church was organized with 26 persons on 21 March 1925. In the beginning, there was some opposition from the local people of village Chaura, but from the same village, one young boy accepted Lord Jesus Christ as personal savior. His name was Murat (Pastor Emmanuel Das). Later on, his mother, two elder, and one young brother became Christians. In the same year, a Primary School for girls was started. The recognition of this School was accorded in 1928. Later on, this school was raised to Junior High School. The girls who could not study further were put in an Industrial school to learn housekeeping, cooking, and plain & fancy needlework.

Miss. Erna Cederholm and Miss Ruth Peterson came to India in 1948. Miss. Cederholm started the Dispensary, but later on took charge of the Mission Station and Hostel. Miss. Peterson worked in Dispensary till she left for Nepal to work as a nurse with the United Mission to Nepal. Miss. Lisa Arnshelem came in 1950, and being a nurse, she worked in a Dispensary for sometime at Chauri Chaura.

Miss. Y. Johansson came to Deoria in 1960 but very soon moved to Chauri Chaura in 1961 and, being a nurse, worked in the Dispensary, then worked as Station-in-charge-Chauri Chaura, and finally became the Field Secretary of Orebro Mission till her retirement in 1994. In the meantime, Miss. Gonvie and Miss. Solvi also came to Chauri Chaura to help Miss. Johansson for some years.

Indian workers who served at Chauri Chaura were Mr. Prem Das, Pastor Emmanuel Gunnar, Pastor James John, Pastor Lachhan Lal, Pastor J. Frankey, Pastor Emmanuel Das, Pastor E. Daniel, Mr. Peter Singh, Pastor T. Mathews, and presently Pastor N. Suman is working.

Tamkuhi Road

Tamkuhi Road was an outstation of Deoria station for some years in the beginning. The actual Mission work was started in the year 1930. A piece of land was given to the Mission by the Estate Superintendent of Babnowlie concern, Tamkuhi Road, on condition that a trained nurse or midwife be posted there to give medical assistance to the local people. The first building in the compound was erected and dedicated on 26th August, 1930. The work prospered and on 11th October, 1931, a Church was organized. Housing accommodation for Mission workers, the Church building, and other facilities necessary for the Mission work at the station followed in due time. Miss Agnes Wallen was the pioneer Missionary. She, along with Indian Evangelists and Bible women, spread the gospel to several people of the villages who accepted Christ as their personal Saviour. After sometime Miss Helga Modigh was stationed at the Tamkuhi mission and used to preach in the villages on her bicycle.

By her great work and spirit, she received Kaiser-i-Hind by the British Government.

Since Tamkuhi Road was a small place and many people moved to other big cities for their livelihood, the membership in the Church had not increased as it should have.But later, a land was taken from the Scottish Sugar factory, and a mission compound was erected. But due to the resistance of the majority community, the baptisms were halted. The mission was warned by the factory owners not to conduct any baptisms due to regional tensions. Otherwise, the land will be taken away from the mission.

In addition to the land on which the Mission compound was built, more land was bought, which was used for the cultivation of wheat and other food grains. Later on, in 1973, a full-fledged 'Christian Leprosy Hospital' was started with the grants given by Leprosy

Mission, Sweden, with the roofing of asbestos sheets. In the year 2008, another grant was received from InterAct, Sweden, for the renovation of the Hospital. Now the Hospital is running with a new look and treating the Leprosy patients of eastern U.P., Bihar, and Nepal. The dependents of the patients are being given tailored training for their rehabilitation. A shoe-making machine is also set up and is doing well. Besides, Leprosy patients, general patients are also being treated. The Mission work at Tamkuhi Road has always been appreciated by the people and the Government.

At present, it is recognized as one of the best Leprosy Hospitals by "The Leprosy Mission', India.

Padrauna

Padrauna stands at 36° 54' N. and 83° 59' E., on the road from Captainganj to Bansighat and Bethiah, at a distance of 12 miles north-north-east by road from Kasia and 49 miles from Gorakhpur.

Padrauna has been an outstation of Deoria for a long time since 1917. The evangelist work was being carried on from Deoria, both by Missionaries and Indian evangelists.

Some of the missionaries used to spend some time during winter in a camp at this place and thus spread the gospel of salvation near Padrauna.

In the year 1938, Rev. & Mrs. Ragnar Gustavsson, a Swedish Missionary couple, came to India and bought a piece of land on the outskirts of Padrauna. He built a Mission Banglow, a preacher's quarter, and a small church attached to the preacher's quarter. These missionaries worked very hard preaching the gospel around Padrauna. They had opened two outposts of Padrauna station, one at Captanganj and another at Kathkunya. From Captanganj, Mr. Mirza Beg accepted Lord Jesus Christ as his personal Savior. He worked as an Evangelist at various Mission stations. Mr. Narain Das worked as Pioneer Evangelist at Padrauna, and Mr. Bental at Kathunya.

Later on, Pastor J. Frankey came to Padrauna and worked there for a long period. Rev. & Mrs. Gustavsson started a small school in the year 1959 before going back to Sweden. Mrs. S. Frankey looked after this school. Rev. Gustavsson did not come back to India but went to Pakistan to work among Muslims. He established several Churches in Pakistan and took his last breath there.

In 1967, Miss A. Hogstad, a Norwegian Missionary along with her daughter Miss 1. Thomas came to Padrauna. Miss Hogstad was not only a Missionary but a visionary too. She took more interest in the all-around development of the work and the community. She bought a piece of land near the church graveyard for the construction of a new School building in 1975, another piece of land near the Mission campus for the construction of the teacher quarters in 1977-78, and for a new Church building in 1986-87.

Miss Thomas took charge of the School in 1973, and now the School is being upgraded to High School in 2004, and the process of recognition for Intermediate classes is going on. An English medium school has also been running simultaneously since 1986. After the retirement of Miss Thomas, her daughter, Mrs. Grace Bezaleel, is working as Principal of the School and is doing well.

Since 1917, evangelistic work has been carried on from this place both by missionaries and evangelists. As the work here has been supervised from Deoria, some of the missionaries from this station have spent some time during the cold weather in camps. Several of the missionaries have been had during some Cold seasons from the records which have appeared in our mission paper from time to time. There is a primary school for Hindu and Muslims boys and girls where the children are taught in reading, writing, and arithmetic with the addition of scripture lessons.

There is also a dispensary at this station. At the very beginning, each missionary began at once the work of preaching in his station, either personally through an interpreter or through the Hindustani helper. People who heard the preaching. In the Bazaar, were impressed by the words that came to the Mission station to make further enquiries.

Anand Nagar

Nils H. Hansson

After 1920, a number of Swedish Missionaries came to India. At one time there were twelve Missionaries and had only two Mission Stations i.e., Barhaj and Deoria. So they started work at new stations, i.e., Barhalganj and Chauri Chaura. In this sequence one new Missionary Mr. Nils Hansson arrived in 1924 and married Miss Signe

Aberg who came to India in 1920 with Rev & Mr. F. B. Rehnstrom. Mr. & Mrs. Hansson moved to Pharenda (now called Anand Nagar) a place near to the border of Nepal. They worked there and established a Church with 9 persons on 24th May, 1931. A Mission Bungalow, quarters for Mission workers and a Church building have been erected at this station. As there has not been any educational and industrial work carried on at this Mission station, the Missionaries.

Pastors, Evangelists and Bible women have been engaged in the direct preaching of the gospel and Christ and in distributing scriptures and tracts.

In addition to the work which was going on in the vicinity of Anand Nagar, evangelistic work was carried on from Basdila, which was an out station of Anand Nagar. There was a congregation and a Church at Basdila, where a self-supporting work was going on. Dispensary work has been carried on for years at this station.

Nils Hansson always wanted to cross the border and spread the word of God in Nepal but his desire remained unfulfilled.

Mr. & Mrs. Hansson worked for quite a long time at Anand Nagar. But, unfortunately, he met with a fatal accident while driving his car on the way to Anand Nagar from Gorakhpur in the year 1955. Record exhibits that Mr. & Mrs. Hansson were the only Missionaries, who worked at Anand Nagar. In the memory of Mr. Hansson a Primary School was opened in 1979 but due to some legal complications, it was closed. Presently, the School building is given on lease to Nav Jeevan Mission Education Trust to run an English medium School.

Indian workers were Mr. Prem Das, Mr. James John, Mr. Prem Masih

Masihi Kalisiya, Gorakhpur

I have been asked to give a brief history of Masihi Kalisiya, Gorakhpur. Though it was a very difficult task to collect the information from various sources, on the other hand, history is supposed to be the most boring subject. Even then, I have tried my level best to do justice with the

responsibility given to me. It is a fact that every individual is eager to know his/her family history. Likewise, every Institution should also know its past. Keeping these facts in mind. I am giving a very short history of Masihi Kalisiya, Gorakhpur, so that you may know the past account of the Church without getting bored.

Rev. C.E. Sjogren was an Evangelist of the Philadelphia Church in Orebro, Sweden. He had a burning desire to come to India with a Gospel message as a Missionary. He shared his desire with Pastor Ongman, the founder of Orebro Mission (Deoria Church is named after Pastor Ongian). Pastor Ongman brought the matter before the Church. The Church decided that Rev CE. Sjogren would be their Missionary Rev. C. E. Sjogren arrived at Kolkata on 3rd November 1908 to select a field for the Mission work. After having spent a few months in consultation with leading local Missionaries, he settled down in Poona. There he felt that he should work among the 'Bhils' in West Khandesh in M.P. He made investigations regarding this field and reported the matter to the Home Board, Sweden for its approval, Unfortunately, no record is preserved of the view expressed by the Board Before anything was finally settled, he fell seriously ill and admitted in J.S. European Central Hospital, Poona, where he took his last breath on 17th October 1910, at the age of 33 years only.

In 1910, two more Missionaries Miss. Lydia Magnusson and Miss. Helga Modig (mother of Mrs Svea Ericksson) came to India. On their arrival in Poona, they came to know that Rev. Sjogren was no more in the world, and nothing was settled about the Mission field. So, the selection of the Mission field was entirely left over to these two ladies. They came in contact with an Indian lady, Mrs. Abraham of Mukti Mission. Mrs. Abraham had to come to Uska Bazar to work as a Bible woman. With her, Miss. Magnusson and Miss. Modig also reached Gorakhpur. Here, they came to know that almost more than one hundred years earlier, Church Mission Society (CMS), England was already working and established various Churches in Gorakhpur, e.g. St. John's Church, Basharatpur (1823), Christ Church, Shastri Chowk (1829), St. Mark's Church, Stempur (1882) and St. Andrew's Church Kauwa Bagh (1898), but rural part was still untouched.

Because of the old principle of Mission Societies that one mission was not allowed to go in to place or district where another mission Society was already working, so they decided to work in the village area, and hence moved to South-eastem corner of Gorakhpur District (Deoria, Kushi Nagar & Maharigani districts of present day were under one District Gorakhpur) called Barhaj Bazar, with a population of about 20,000. They put their feet on the land of Barhaj Bazar on 15th April 1911 and took a very ordinary tile-roofed house on rent on the roadside of the Barhaj-Paina route and stayed there until 1917 when Mission Bungalow was built. As the house belonged to the Raja of Majhauli for his servants who used to collect tax, nobody could buy it due to the litigation of its successor, Miss. Magnusson and Miss. Modig wrote to the House Board, Sweden, for their selection of Barhaj as a mission field, which was later approved by the Board. These Missionaries further contacted Mukti Mission, Poona, to get some Preachers and Bible Women. As a result, Mr. & Mrs. Mohan, Mr. & Mrs. Bapu Powar from Poona, Mrs. Konkarbai from Dhond and Mr. Kuber Lakha from Banaras came to Barhaj. In the meantime, a third Missionary, Mr. Frank Henricksson, landed at Barhaj in November 1911. All these believers met together to worship God and praise Him for the opportunity to present the gospel in an area where no Missionary or Preacher had ever been before.

This small group of Missionaries, Preachers and Bible Women, about 10 persons, established the first Church of this Mission at Barhaj on Easter Sunday, 1912 (7th April 1912).

With the influx of more Missionaries at Barhaj, they felt that there was no need for all of them to live in one place, so some of them moved to different places and established Churches.

Rev. Dr. & Mrs. F. B. Rehnstrom came to Deoria in 1920 and worked there for 17 years. He started a Theological School in 1930, which was shifted to Gorakhpur in 1937 and continued up to 1942

One of the main factors which influenced Rev. & Mrs. F. B. Rehnstrom was being main district of eastern Uttar Pradesh, Gorakhpur provides more job opportunities in Railways workshop & offices, Schools, Hospital etc. to the then generation and future generations, they broke the old principle of Mission Societies and moved to Gorakhpur from Deoria in March 1937 to lay permanent foundation for an indigenous Church at Gorakhpur.

At the same time, Ms. Rajni Bai and Mr. & Mrs. Hira Lal were transferred to Gorakhpur, Rev Rehnstrom took a house adjacent to the present 42- Jail Road, on rent for his residence. Another house was taken in Suri Bagia on rent for residence to Indian workers and a place for worship. After some time, Mr. & Mrs. Emmanuel Das were transferred to Gorakhpur to work with other workers. A piece of land was purchased in 1937, on which the present Church building and house accommodation for the Pastor / Evangelist were erected in 1938. The Church at Gorakhpur was organized on 23rd October

1938 with 23 members. The first pastor ordained here was Ps. Emmanuel Das. He is a skilled preacher and possesses a spirit of wisdom and revelation about God. He has also been often called to larger conferences, including those of an American Pentecostal mission, which considers him one of the foremost spiritual speakers in northern India. Rev. Dr. Rehnstrom bought the present 42-Jail Road Bungalow for the residence of Missionaries. He was the first Missionary and visionary who established a church outside the Mission compound (Missionary Bungalow), so that Church activities may not be influenced by Missionaries.

In the year 1945, Rev. Dr. Rehnstrom bought another piece of land on the eastern side, just in front of the then Church Compound, in which the approach road and main gate were built, which leads to the main road.

After a very long and sincere service, Rev. Dr. and Mrs. Rehnstrom retired and retürned to Sweden in 1957. In 1967, they visited this Mission field. He said, "When I saw the grace of God, I rejoiced and glorified His name. I found that the Churches had multiplied and were edified and walked in the fear of the Lord, and in the comfort of the Holy Spirit". Other Missionaries who worked at Gorakhpur were Rev. & Mrs. Jean Malm (1957-1962), Miss. H. Andersson, Rev. & Mrs. Bengt Jonsson (1962-1965), Rev. & Mrs. Evert Ericksson (1965-1985), Mrs.

Solevi John came to Gorakhpur in 1972 to work among children, youth, and women. The Indian workers who worked at Gorakhpur were Mrs. Rajni Bai, Mr. & Mrs. Hira Lal, Pastor & Mrs. Emmanuel Das (Pastor Eamanuel Das was first ordained Pastor of this Church), Pastor & Mrs. S. Lawrence, Mr. Daya Din, Mr. Prem Masih, Mr. Misri Lal, Pastor J. T. Peter, Pastor S. Isaiah , Pastor G. P. Dutt, Pastor Victor John, Mr. Suresh Massey, Mr. Ranjit Lal, Pastor Kailash Sharma, Pastor Khrishtvir Singh, Pastor Surjit Das and Pastor J. P. Singh. Presently, Pastor R. John and Acting Pastor Shobhit Solomon are serving.

Here I would like to mention that on the occasion of the Platinum Jubilee Celebration of the Church on 23 October 2013, the foundation stone of the extension of the Church building on both wings was laid and it was opened on 23rd October 2014 Mrs. S. Ericksson started Mission School in the church compound in 1968, with the assistance of Mrs. S. Lal, for the poor and needy Christian children. But later on, it was opened for all. The Proper School building was erected in 1986 with her efforts. Presently, it is running up to class VII under the guidance of Mrs. Shyama L. Das.

Genesis of CMS

CMS Parsonage (1823)

The Church Mission Society story began more than 200 years ago with a group of Christians whose hearts were stirred to go to the edges.

The Society was founded in Aldersgate Street in the City of London on 12 April 1799. The group included people like William Wilberforce, John Venn, and John Newton. Together, they worked to abolish the slave trade, they fought for the rights of oppressed people at home, and they launched out onto dangerous seas to share Jesus with the world.

Mr. Robert Merttins Bird (CMS) was the additional district Magistrate of Gorakhpur, and he cared about the Anglo Indians very much.

He was the key person to establish the Church Missionary Society in Gorakhpur and his sister Mary Bird came here to assist him, learned Hindustani, and worked for the CMS mission.

Narratives of Michael Wilkinson, the missionary –

MR. WILKINSON'S immediate successor was the late devoted, able, and energetic Secretary of the Calcutta Corresponding Committee, the Rev. Frederick Wybrow. He was in every respect a man of kindred spirit, and one well fitted for the laborious and important post of Missionary, Evangelist and Pastor in the district of Gorruckpore. He joined the mission in 1840, shortly before Mr. Wilkinson's departure, and in a few months commenced preaching in Hindustani, having before that only been imperfectly acquainted with Bengali.

A brief sketch of his bright Christian career has been drawn up by his widow, with a preface by the Rev. R. Boswell, above referred to. As stated, Mr. Wybrow had not laboured more than six months before he caught the fatal jungle fever, from imprudently sleeping on the banks of the mission tank, and was a corpse in a few hours.At that time, about thirty acres of the farm were kept under cultivation by native Christian boys, who were accustomed to work in the early morning, then go to school till the afternoon, and then again engage in labour till sunset. The rearing of the sugar-cane had been introduced by Mr. W., but was given up in consequence of the depredations of the wild elephants. This amount of land, cultivated by the native Christian lads, was in addition to several hundred acres, cultivated by thirty Christian families.

After Mr. Wybrow's death, in December 1840, the Rev. Messrs. Wendragle and J. P. Menge, from Basle, were appointed to the mission. Mr. Wendragle, after labouring with indifferent health and but partial success at the "Farm," where he resided, returned homeward, but died on board ship; and Mr. Menge was left alone in charge of the whole mission, includ-ing the "Farm" itself, and the European station, where, besides the Europeans, the native Christian teachers connected with the large boys' and girls' schools were located. Mr. Menge was ably seconded and supported by the native catechist above mentioned, Charles Dass, who has laboured most faithfully and formed the connecting link between the various missionary pastors and the native flock collected in the wilderness by one and another of the ordained missionaries. Mr. Menge early adopted the plan of catechising the native Christians, in the week, upon the subject of the previous Sunday's sermon.

It does not appear that much further progress was made for some time made, in bringing under cultivation the large tract of land secured by Mr. Wilkinson's exertions and Lord W. Bentinck's liberality. But until the late outbreak, the Christian village and adjacent farm were maintained in a flourishing condition under Mr. Menge's judicious superintendence, with the aid of a resident native catechist.

The writer can testify to the pleasure which he derived some years after, from a visit to his native place, in company with one now no more. The sight of the faithful missionary pastor, alone in a district as large as Scotland, surrounded by an intelligent, though humble congregation of native Christians, (whom he himself had the privilege of addressing, in the Church in the

Wilderness), besides a smaller one in the station Church; both these churches rising in the midst of missionary bungalows, (of which alas! but one was tenanted,) and surrounded by the large schools erected by Messrs. Bird and Tucker, and other active and philanthropic civil and military servants of the H. E. I. C. (Honorable East India Company) the coup d'œuil of the pastor at the head of his little flocks, and the pretty bungalows and school houses, surrounded by the neat mud cottages and well-tended gardens and fields of the native Christians,all reclaimed from a dense and pestiferous jungle, and the former redeemed from the still more fearful moral wilderness around: this scene, with the beauty of the station, and the wild tropical scenery, (trying and dangerous though it is to European constitutions), altogether left an impression on the mind which time will never obliterate. Would there be many more such scenes in India? Mr. Menge's pastoral duties prevented his itinerating at first to the extent that he could have wished, and which the less advanced state of the mission in Mr. Wilkinson's time rendered more practicable. Still, we gather from the Annual Reports of the Society, that besides preaching daily in the bazaars, Mr. Menge frequently visited the neighbouring Hindu and Muslim shrines and Melâs, distributing tracts, besides orally disseminating the seeds of the blessed Gospel.

Thus, in 1846, the missionary "Held many conversations on the subject of religion with the Mahomedans." He finds "that if one comes, he listens with much greater attention than if several are present." This, of course, arises from the inquisitorial system of priestly domination, in which they, in common with all false and superstitious religionists, are held, and of which Popish countries can alone furnish any counterpart. Still, "the Hindus," writes Mr. M., "are on the whole far more inclined to listen with pleasure to the Gospel than the Mussulmans." This year we read that Mr. Menge preached in thirty-eight different villages, and remarked, "I have found great simplicity in poor villagers, especially if removed from the corrupting influence of large towns."

About the schools. The English school, established in 1835 (after a meeting convened by the principal European and native inhabitants), in 1850 exceeded one hundred in number, and in 1852, the total number of children under education in the four schools in connection with the society amounted to two hundred and sixty-five. Of these, some fifteen or sixteen were girls belonging to the female girls' school, commenced by Mrs. Wilkinson in 1824, continued by Miss Bird, and carried on under the careful superintendence of Mrs. Menge. Although the ultimate success of missions is not to be measured entirely by the number of baptized converts, yet this is, after all, the chief object of the missionary's aspirations. It is therefore interesting to note the various means which the Holy Spirit employs to bring about this great object. There is an interesting instance of this, effected through Mr. Menge's labours, and which originated (like that of the "Old Sheikh," the Mahomedan convert of Mr. Wilkinson's), in reading the Holy Scriptures, which opened his eyes to the sin of idolatry. The case referred to is that of Baldeo, a native doctor. A copy of the New Testament had been given him by a pious chaplain of the H. E. I. C.(Honorable East India Company) at Allahabad. For two years, he attended the preaching of the missionary in the bazaar of the city, besides seeking frequent private interviews. His mother, wife, two brothers, and a servant who lived with him, were all brought to a knowledge of the truth, and apparently sincere conversion to the faith of the Gospel, and were baptized in the name of Jesus. This took place in 1851. Baldeo died shortly afterwards, and when visited on his death-bed by the missionary, and questioned by him as to the sufficiency of the hope that was in him, roused himself to reply, "Oh yes, with every breath I breathe, I breathe the holy name of Jesus."

Baldeo was a man of learning and had commenced to write a poem in Hindustani, in praise of his Saviour and the blessings of Christianity when arrested by the cold hand of death.

Nevertheless, "he being dead yet speak," for his brother, one of the fruits of his own conversion, is now a zealous preacher of the Gospel. His wife, too, proved an intelligent, enlightened Christian.

It was not long after this (in 1852) that a body of agriculturists who had till then "seen but not believed," convinced of the truth of Christianity, embraced the religion of Jesus, and settled on the farm at Basharat-pore, which continued "prospering in every respect, and yielding a considerable surplus." The latter Mr. Menge expanded in clearing fresh jungle, and extending the Christian village. This year, he continued his itinerant preaching tours and was in consequence, visited by a considerable number of persons, especially Zemindars (landowners) and Pundits in the neighbourhood. In fact, for weeks in succession, he had more than forty visitors each week. So mightily had the seed of the Word of God, sown by Mr. Menge and his predecessor, Mr. Wilkinson, already begun to "grow and prevail."

The congregation now amounted to two hundred and seventeen souls, and the children under education in the several schools and orphan institutions exceeded three hundred. Still, it may be asked, "What are they among so many," or, as Mr. M. truly and affectingly remarks, "I leave the committee to judge what permanent impression can be made on a district that contains two and a half million of inhabitants, by one missionary of the cross."

At the commencement of the year, this station was visited by Archdeacon Pratt, who reports, "At Gorruckpore and in the district around, many respectable natives are coming in to the missionary from week to week, and from day to day, saying, they have heard him preaching in their villages, or have heard others speaking of him, and enquiring the way of God more perfectly." Again at the close of the year, the station was visited by the Rev. G. G. Cuthbert, secretary to the Calcutta Corresponding Committee, who bears testimony to the "thriving and pleasing aspect" of the mission, and "the spirit of enquiry" which still appeared to continue.

But meanwhile, the devoted missionary's health had given way, after nearly twelve years of almost uninterrupted labours, and two successors had been appointed, the Rev. Messrs. Kreiss from Agra and Rev. H. Stern from Benares. The former was, after eighteen months' labours "suddenly cut down by death in June, 1855; consequently the whole care of the mission has ever since rested upon one missionary (the Rev. H. Stern)," then a young unmarried man, who has, how-ever, proved himself no stripling in the discharge of duties, and the endurance of trials, this Honour, the late Mr. Colvin, Lieut. Governor, N. W. P., who distributed the prizes.

In this school, Persian and Hindi as well as English are the languages taught; and at the previous examination, as on the present occasion, great credit was given to the teachers and superintendent by the civil and military officers, who kindly examined the boys. His Honour also visited Basharatpore, and attended divine service there (in the Church in the Wilderness) with the native Christians, "kneeling side by side with them to worship God in His sanctuary, and joining with them in the same responses of our beautiful liturgy." *

Shortly before, another school, erected by the magistrate, Mr. Paterson, had been made over to the Church Missionary Society. It was already filled with one hundred boys.

During the year 1855, the late Bishop of Calcutta visited the Gorruckpore mission, and was met by about twenty native Christian families at the entrance to the church, where they were addressed by his Lordship, Mr. Stern interpreting. After that, they entered the village, and paid a few visits to the Christians' houses, (which seemed, though humble and poor, in good order,) with their little stores of grain *He has now (it is firmly hoped), exchanged the communion of saints on earth for that of the Church Triumphant above. To say the least, second to none experienced by his predecessors.

With the aid of two experienced native catechists, one of whom conducted daily service at the "farm," whilst the other assisted at the station, "the work," writes Mr. S., "has been carried on as usual. Three adult Hindus were added during the year to the Church of Christ, and some inquirers are constantly coming in."

In December 1855, the English school, containing some two hundred and thirty boys, was examined by and plots of land close by, Mr. Stern observes, "the farm appeared well cultivated and very fertile, though needing effective superintendence, with the aid of which they would soon form a thriving community, and an example to others." The Christian Girls' School was examined and found to have improved. The Large Boys' School also showed a decided advance since 1854. Most of the native Christian boys were taught with the Hindus and Muslims in the school.

But this fair and favoured spot was soon to be marred and devastated by the ruthless hands of fiends in human form, who, with the name of religion on their lips, and under the pretext of a thousand imaginary, and some few real grievances, let loose the hell hounds of lust, rapine, and bloodshed over this and many another scene of British and missionary enterprize. Things went on much the same during the ensuing year. The solitary missionary held on his quiet yet steady course of progress, "Not able to relate great success, yet not discouraged." But early in the following year, 1857, the distant sounds of the impending storm became louder and more threatening, till all at once it burst upon them with terrific violence.

Mr. Stern thus writes, January 10th, 1858, "This time I am spared the task of relating in detail what we have been doing, our experiences, our successes, our failures; and indeed this may well be dispensed with,for much of what we have been doing, and we hope all that was unprofitable and sinful, has been buried beneath the ruins of India as it was. Futurity only will reveal India as it will be, for most assuredly she will go forth out of this fearful struggle between Heathenism and Mahommedanism on the one hand, and Christianity on the other, better prepared to receive the Gospel, which she has so long and so obstinately rejected.

How a village of glad tiding became village of weeping and then turned to a town of joy!

"Up to the 13th of August, the various branches of the mission were carried on as usual. We considered it a special cause for thanksgiving that, notwithstanding the great and many dangers to which we were continually exposed, church service and school were carried on without interruption up to the very day before we were called upon by the authorities to quit the station. It was," he proceeds, "a very sad sight, thus in one long procession to leave the station (in charge of the Goorkhas), and I could not help thinking of King David, when he, with his nobles, fled from his son Absalom." The schools were closed the day before, and placed with the whole mission, including Basharatpore, the farm, and all the native Christians, under the care of the friendly Hindu Rajah of Gopalpur. A few accompanied the Europeans as servants; the rest, one hundred and sixty-two in number, were left to the guardian care of "that Great Shepherd of the Sheep," by whose loving-kindness they had been, after so many years of labour, and prayers, and tears, gathered together in this dark land."

Rev. Henry Stern's last visit to the village of "Glad Tidings" was a sad one. It might rather have been called the village of "weeping." The villagers assembled in the house of the catechist, where he read the 71st Psalm and prayed, commending them to Him in whom they had believed.

Thus was the faithful missionary fain to leave his "few sheep in the wilderness." But his prayers were not unanswered, for though they were soon scattered and had to flee from the fold, rather than submit to the demands of the Mussulmans that they should renounce their religion, the friendly Rajah having been deposed by these intruders, they were, except one of the native catechists, (a convert of Rev. Michael Wilkinson's), spared the horrors of a massacre. They left Basharatpore after enduring for two months the persecutions of their infidel oppressors, on the 20th of October, 1857. After breaking up into small parties and running the gauntlet of robbers and plunderers of all descriptions, they escaped with "their lives for a prey" and in a state of extreme destitution to Aligunje, near Chupra, one hundred and forty-one in number. Here, after some few weeks, they were once more joined by their afflicted yet joyful pastor; and shortly after, on the re-occupation of Gorruckpore by the Goorkhars, (who had been compelled to leave it on proceeding to protect Juanpore), the little flock, somewhat reduced in numbers, yet praising God for their wonderful preservation, returned with its shep-herd to their ruined and desolate abodes. Their immediate wants had meanwhile been liberally met by the Relief Fund Committee.

In conclusion, we would most heartily echo the prayer of one, to whom, as well as to her late husband, the Church of Christ owes much, that "after peace are restored to the disturbed provinces, by God's blessing on the British arms, Basharatpore will become more emphatically than ever a **town of joy**,' and its Church in the Wilderness' will be surrounded by a fruitful field."

The impact of the Revolt (1857)

This story dates back to 1857, when the first war of independence had begun. It was led by Muhammad Hasan, but after the British victory, he was removed from his position. This fueled a burning resentment in his heart. Gorakhpur came under British rule in 1801. At that time, Saadat Ali Khan was the Nawab of Awadh. Following this, English officers were appointed to the district, including the first Collector, Patterson, and Judge Vinyard. When the rebellion began in 1857,

R.M. Bird was the Joint Magistrate here. In this struggle, Muhammad Hasan was supported by Babu Bandhu Singh, the ruler of Dumri. Raja Harprasad of Narharpur, the Raja of Rudrapur, and Raja Paramhans Singh of Siswa also provided their support. At that time, almost all the The British had left the district, but Bird was still in charge. He believed that the Mughal Nazim would not attack his area because of his honesty. The betrayal came when Musharraf Khan arrived at his bungalow at Board Ghat with his soldiers, who were imprisoned in the jail. He sat down on the sofa in Bird's room and informed Bird that whatever accounts they had between them were now settled, and he challenged him to a fight. After saying this, he left the bungalow, warning him that he would return. Bird then sent a letter to the Gurkha contingent, but receiving no reply, his anxiety deepened. Seeing himself alone, Bird managed to escape on his elephant through the jungle towards Chhapra. The date of this battle is the beginning of June. According to Colonel Lennox, when he arrived in Gorakhpur by boat from Ayodhya at 2:00 PM with his family, some men on the bank informed him that a group of Europeans had passed through here looking for them, and they warned him to go to a safe place quickly. As they were leaving, a soldier on horseback, armed with weapons, spotted them. Upon seeing him, the group of men quickened their pace. However, he approached them, offered them water, and assured them of safe passage to a secure location. It appeared that Muhammad Hasan's fort was some distance away. Immediately afterwards, 10-12 other soldiers arrived and provided us with protection.

They instructed us to walk in a certain direction. One of the soldiers said loudly, "I wish I could riddle these arrogant men with bullets; they are converting our brothers and sisters to Christianity." Upon reaching the fort, we were taken care of. Nazim met with us and assured us of protection. But our companions on another boat, who were about to reach Gorakhpur after escaping from Azamgarh, were pursued by a rebel group. They tried to escape on foot after abandoning the boat, but they were caught and killed. Another account is from Mahadeva Bazaar near Bansgaon, where a group of rebels murdered our unfortunate companions. Here, some of our companions, including Lindsay, Cautley, Thomas, and Ritchie, perished. Sergeant Major Busher managed to escape. Another detachment (O'Brien, Gordon, Collison, Anderson, and Pereival) somehow reached Gorakhpur from Ayodhya by changing boats. There, the Raja of Gopalpur gave them protection. The Raja of Gopalpur, Kishan Kishore Chand, was heavily in debt. Goldney also recounts that while he was coming from Faizabad towards Gorakhpur, the rebel Balli Singh captured him on the way. However, being near Badhpur, Mr. P.P. (the estate manager) sent a sub-inspector to fetch me. Before this, Collector Patterson and the indigo planter Mr. Cook had also tried to rescue me. Upon reaching there, I was very happy to meet Mr. Peppe and Colonel Lennox. After staying in Basti Badhpur, Colonel Lennox and I departed for Gorakhpur. A letter states: "We are now under the protection of the honest Raja of Gopalpur." Gopalpur is 120 km from Gorakhpur. Present here are our colleagues

Captain Reed, Mrs. Orr, Mrs. Thurburn, Mr. & Mrs. Dawson, Mr. & Mrs. Bedford, Mr. & Mrs. Fitzgerald, and Mr. and Mrs. Hurst. The second account concerns the village of Basharatpur, where there is a description of the persecution and expulsion of the local Christians. The church in Basharatpur is also destroyed. People's homes are attacked. Grain, money, goods, and livestock are looted. The pastor there, Henry Stern, spends the night and the next day departs for Aliganj by boat. He manages to escape with some of the residents. However, the Christian residents (Tobit, Obadiah, Frank, Newbolt, Sulaiman Beson, and Timothy) were imprisoned.

Catechist-In-charge Rapheal (St. John's Cemetery)

(The descendants of the imprisoners are still present in the locality).Naib Musharraf Khan's soldiers arrive there and kill the catechist in charge, Raphael, and inquire about Bird. Bird's sister, Mary, was working as a missionary in Basharatpur. Raphael is beaten and killed.

Muhammad Hasan's rule lasted for approximately six months. Initially, Patterson wanted to come from Azamgarh to Gorakhpur, but Kunwar Singh of Jagdishpur and his seventy-year-old brother, Amar Singh, blocked his path. According to Dr. Darkhshan Tajwar's article, the jailer of Motijail, Muhammad Ibrahim, himself goes to the opposite bank to welcome Muhammad Hasan and his revolutionary companions. The list includes Musharraf Pandit, Sardar Ali, Ali Hasan, Naunidh Rai, Mirza, Fateh Ali, Muhammad Saeed, Abid Hussain, Ulfat Ali, Amir Ali, Guma Khan, Imdad Ali, Mazhar Ali, Wahid Ali, Ahmad Khan, Kallu Beg, Brijmohan, Anup, and Shakarullah.Mansoor Ali, Makhdoom Baksh, and Faiz accompanied him. Before Mohammad Hasan reached Gorakhpur, Musharraf Ali Madar Baksh and some of his companions had arranged for the treasury, cannons, and supplies. The revolutionaries burned down the Board's office, but did not damage any other government offices or offices. Meanwhile, the jailer of Moti Jail, Agha Mohammad Ibrahim, released the prisoners. The British fought a major battle at the Lal Diggi Dam near Moti Jail.

Ultimately, Mohammad Hasan and the revolutionaries won.

Mohammad Hasan himself assumed the position of Nazim and appointed Musharraf Khan as his deputy Nazim. Mohammad Hasan's rule was also approved by the government of Awadh. He was honored with the title of Mukarribuddaula and a robe. According to the Mission in Gorakhpur, gifts were also offered to the nazim because Mohammad Hasan had liberated the district from the British, but Christians refused to offer any valuables. Under the leadership of Babu Bandhu Singh, Mohammad Hasan looted the government treasury, formed his own government, and in his first order, repealed all laws enacted by the British. Hasan collected revenue, established a court, and, after assuming power, formed his own army. The army consisted primarily of Nawaban, Gauhar, Shamsher Ali, Ehsan Ali, Khurshid Ali, Waziran, Kallu Beg, Hasan Khan, Ramphal, Ghiyasuddin Khan, and his son Dildar Khan, Walidar Khan, Chinghe Khan, Narayan, and Abid Ali. Approximately 25,000 men were recruited. On December 26, 1857, a major battle took place in Sohanpur between Colonel Rowcroft's army and Mohammad Hasan's. Another clash also broke out in Basharatpur, as evidenced by the tomb of the martyr Mirza Ghalib, located on the other side of the pond. On January 6, 1858, a contingent of Rana Jung

Bahadur of Nepal, led by McGregor, reached Gorakhpur. Additionally, armed forces arrived due to the British's friendship with the rebels. On January 11, 1858, a fierce battle ensued with the revolutionaries. A large number of patriots were martyred on this occasion.

Mohammad Hasan left for Tanda with his companions. A major reason for Mohammad Hasan's departure was that before the attack, he had been in Tanda to arrange for the money tax. During this period, he had assisted Colonel Lennox and his family. After the British reestablishment, a large number of revolutionaries were hanged. The main execution sites were Alinagar, Ghantaghar, and Moti Jail. The British hanged Mohammad Hasan's deputy, Musharraf Khan, in Alinagar. In this series, Rasul Ali, Aulad Ali, Naunidh Rai, and Wahid Ali are confirmed to have been hanged. Information also exists about the executions of Basant Nath, Tuman's soldier Lal Khan, Sheikh Faizu, Walidad Khan, Karimdad Khan, Inayat Ali, and Hyder Hussain. The Motijheel Committee has two graves dedicated to the martyrs of the Ganjhe community in the Saudagar Mohalla cemetery. A large number of revolutionaries belonging to this neighborhood are buried in these graves In continuation of the narratives of Rev. H. Stern this mission was under the charge of the Rev. H. Stern, missionary of the Church Missionary Society, who was also the acting minister of the church in which the residents of the station assembled for Divine worship. Two large schools were in connection with the mission. The one was a boarding school for the children of native Christians, and for orphans, both male and female, and contained a large number of pupils. The other school was for natives and had one hundred and sixty scholars. Besides these, there were also two schools in the bazaar. In addition, the mission had the superintendence of a village in the neighbourhood of Gorruckpore, in which many of the native Christians resided, having each a small portion of land which they cultivated, and from the proceeds of which they subsisted. The name of the village was Basharatpore.

This station was first exposed to danger, not only from within, but also from without. The troops in the cantonments were detachments from the Azimghur infantry and the Segowlie cavalry regiments, both of which mutinied early in June. It is needless to remark, therefore, that from the moment of the mutiny at their headquarters, the sepoys in Gorruckpore became most villainously inclined. The proximity of the city to Oude was an additional source of danger. On the arrival of six regiments of Goorkhas from Nepal, the sepoys were disarmed, and shortly after,

they all disappeared except about fifty men. As only eight hundred Goorkhas were to be left in Gorruckpore, the local authorities, thinking the force totally insufficient for the defence of the place, deemed it expedient to abandon the station. They all departed, with the entire body of the Goorkhas, for Azimghur and Jaunpore; first taking over the station and district to the care of several loyal rajahs, who promised to do their best to protect both, and to preserve them in order. It was necessary that Mr Stern, if he had the least desire of saving his life, should accompany the other residents. There was no second course open to him, for it would have been sheer madness to remain behind. It must have been with a sad spirit that the missionary quitted the scene of his labours, which in all probability was speedily to be spoliated by the ruthless hand of a cruel enemy.

How painful, too, must it have been to bid adieu to the native Christians, especially as the future appeared so dark and threatening. Truly, this was a moment to try the steadfastness of the bravest heart. Before leaving, Mr

Stern placed the native Christians under the protection of a rajah in the neighbourhood, who had always displayed a friendly feeling towards the mission.

The rajah was promised the reward of a year's relief of land-tax payable to the Government, in consideration of his affording such protection.

The residents left, and the station was soon taken possession of by the rebel chief, Mohammed Hussain. It was not long before the poor native Christians were exposed to ill-treatment from this chief and from his cruel myrmidons. The rajah was unable or unwilling to defend them.

They were robbed of nearly everything. They were savagely beaten. Their women were abused. Their bullocks were taken from them. Driven from their fields, they were reduced to the greatest extremities. Mohammed Hussain threatened that if they did not become Mussulmans they would all be killed. It was wisely considered better to make their escape from such heavy persecutions, even though they might have to encounter great trials in the attempt. They therefore made arrangements to go away, a few at a time, to avoid observation, which by God's providence enabled them to carry out. They fled through the jungles across the country to Aligunj, which was in the hands of the Government, and was some eighty or one hundred miles distant from Gorruckpore. From this place, they communicated with Mr Stern, who was now residing in Benares. On receiving the news of their safe arrival at Aligunj, Mr. Stern left in a boat for that place. The affecting story of the meeting of the native Christians with their missionary, I leave to Mr. Stern himself to tell.

Narrative of the Rev. II. Stern, respecting his interview with the escaped Native Christians from Gorruckpore.

Aligunj, Sewan, Sarun District, Nov. 23, 1857.

"I arrived here safely on Thursday last, and found all the native Christians from Gorruckpore well, except several fever cases. The native Christians, no less than I, were very happy to see each other again, after a separation of upwards of three months. Before I came up to them, where they were encamped, in a large mango grove, the children came out running to meet me, and to conduct me into the midst of their parents, who soon surrounded me. Everyone now commenced to tell his tale of the late trials and privations, in which all took an equal share. We all then had prayers to thank the good Lord and Shepherd of our souls, for thus having preserved and saved us from many dangers, and for having given us this fresh token of mercy, in permitting us thus to meet again. To Him be all praise and glory!

"The Christians left Basharatpore on the 20th of October. For upwards of two months (the station of Gorruckpore was abandoned on the 13th of August), they lived in continual fear and anxiety, being exposed to the spoliation of their goods and to personal ill-treatment. During a dacoity, one of the Christians received a deep sword-cut in his back; others were beaten; the women, who usually ran into the jungle, were abused; and the catechist in charge, Raphael,seems to have been particularly exposed to the fury of the enemy. The maltreatment that he received very much hastened his death, which happened on the 12th of October. A few days after this, their best bullocks were seized, and several of the men were carried before the Chakladar, who kept them prisoners for two days. On learning that they were Christians, he ordered them to deny their faith and become Muslims. One of the Chakladar's men then interfered and said that these Christians had been neither Hindus nor Mussulmans but were brought up as orphans in the Christian religion, and would therefore not be received by either of these persuasions.

"Nevertheless, the Chakladar insisted on their becoming Mohammedans, and requested them to look out for a Moulvie. Seven Christians, as they tell me, pretended to consent to this arrangement. Upon this, they were allowed to go to their homes. When they got there, they told their brethren what had happened. They then consulted together about what to do. That very day, they all resolved to quit the place, especially as also on the previous day a Mussulman, belonging to the Chakladar's suite, had come to Basharatpore, and told the people that they had been great fools for remaining behind, when the Europeans left the station; advising them to leave Basharatpore at once quietly, as evil was intended against them. They therefore left in small parties by stealth at night, during several successive days, the last party leaving on the 20th October, after they had agreed to meet in a place called Shahpore, to the east of Gorruckpore, and beyond the boundary of that district. They all took the road through the jungle, and, after three days' travelling, they reached Shahpore in safety, only one party having been robbed on the road; the others saved a few clothes, and some even escaped with their carts and pair of bullocks. Shahpore, not being far from Bettiah, a Roman Catholic establishment, three families went there for protection; the rest intended to go to Benares. Having come so far as Aligunj, they wrote to me about their doings; and a magistrate, Mr Lynch, being stationed here, they applied to him for assistance. This gentleman wrote to me, and in the meantime exerted himself on their behalf with the officers and men of the Naval Brigade, who had then just arrived, and I am happy to say that his exertions have been most successful, for both men and officers took a warm interest in their welfare. Mr. Lynch has been very kind to them also in other ways; he has given them the use of a tent, for the accommodation of the sick and the infant portion, and has taken ten men into his employ as chowkedars.

"They also found a warm friend in the Rev. Mr Williams, the chaplain attached to the Naval Brigade, whom I had the happiness to meet here on my arrival, and who got employment for several of them with some of the officers. Before I arrived here, they were once visited by a catechist, who was sent out by the missionaries in Chuprah, and afterwards again were visited and relief afforded them by Dr Ribbentrop, the devoted and self-denying missionary of the Chuprah mission."Mr M'Donald, deputy opium-agent and acting magistrate, has kindly undertaken to apply to the Relief Fund in Calcutta on their behalf, as our little private fund is exhausted, and there are about one hundred and fifty souls for whom to provide. Both Mr. M'Donald and Mr. Lynch belong to the Roman Catholic persuasion; the more credit, therefore, it does these gentlemen for having taken the part of these Christians."

I have obtained a complete account of the troubles and dangers which the poor Christians of Gorruckpore had to encounter at the hands of the enemy, written by Peter, a catechist of the mission. I think that in no mission throughout the whole of these provinces, except that at Chhota Nagpore, has a greater amount of persecution and suffering been experienced than has fallen to the lot of our native brethren there. Although they were not all equally staunch and did not display the same high moral courage and the same trust in God at all times, yet we have to thank God for the fact that nearly all remained steadfast to their faith, and that none embraced Mohammedanism, notwithstanding that several, when in great danger of their lives, promised to do so. Upwards of one hundred and fifty Christian people, men, women, and children, were for two months plundered, abused, beaten, im-prisoned, threatened with death, and afflicted in a countless variety of ways, and yet they continued firm-yet, with few exceptions, they held fast to Christ they did not purchase liberty by apostasy, and endured all things through Christ that loved them. The Lord be praised!

Peter the Catechist's Narrative of the Persecution of the Gorruckpore Native Christians, and of their Escape to Aligunj.

"On the day that the Europeans intended to leave Gorruckpore, the Rev. H. Stern gave the Christian village of Basharatpore and the native Christians into the charge of the Rajah of Gopalpore. Consequently, the rajah sent some of his own soldiers to guard the village, but these men commenced annoying the Christians. On the Sabbath, when they assembled for prayer in the house of Raphael, the soldiers used to stand looking on with their swords in their hands, and talking aloud. When intelligence arrived that the Chakladar was coming, the rajah recalled his soldiers from the village. When these wicked fellows were leaving, they destroyed a quantity of the mission property and carried various things away with them. After their departure, we had peace and quiet for a few days. When the Chakla-dar had been in the city a short time, several sepoys came into the village, armed with shields, swords, and guns. A number of the brethren were sitting under a tree. Abusing them, they inquired, 'Where is your chief?' They replied, 'He is living in the house there,' pointing it out. The sepoys then came to Raphael's house. On seeing them, the Christians began to collect together. They were then asked, 'Who is the chief man among you?' Raphael said, 'I am.' The sepoys thereupon threatened us, in very coarse and violent language, and said, 'Where have you hidden Mr. Bird? If you don't tell us, we will take your chief before the Chakladar, and, if he resists, we will bind you all and take you before him. We took advice from each other, and concluded that it would not be good to go before the Chakladar, but that we had better give these men something and send them away. So we made a subscription among ourselves, which we gave to them, and, with many entreaties, we got them to leave.

"On the next day, another batch of sepoys made its appearance and seized our oxen, which the men said were needed to drag the cannon. We only ransomed them by a gift of four annas, or sixpence a-head. On the third day, other sepoys came to the village, and their leader ordered that we should all be bound and taken before Musarraf Khan, for that we were very proud and rebellious. He said, moreover, that all the Hindus, and Mussulmans of the neighbourhood had presented gifts to the Chakladar, whereas we had not even gone to pay our respects to him. We again made a subscription and begged not to be taken before the Khan, and they at last left with the money. On the fourth day, very early in the morning, sepoys were again seen in the village. They first of all went into the bungalow and took some things from it. They next went into the stable of Raphael, and carried off his horse. We ran after them to prevent their making off with the animal, but, on approaching them, they pointed their muskets at us; so, out of fear for our lives, we were obliged to leave them with their booty.

"After these troubles, two agents of the Rajah of Sattasee came into the village, bringing with them a great company of sepoys. They plundered the bunga-low, then the church, and after this searched the Christians' houses, each man taking whatever he liked. On the same day, a Mohammedan beat Raphael with the stock of a gun and kicked him with his feet, which he endured very patiently. He had been ill before this, but the beating which he received, added to his sickness and his depression of spirits, was too much for his frame, and he at last sank under his trials. He died on the 12th October 1857. He had been greatly persecuted, for the sepoys always went first to his house; but I have good hope he is now in heaven, as he died in the faith of the gospel.

"Now, as only a few things remained in the possession of the Christians, they themselves began to be seized by the enemy. Some, from fear, fled into the country, and those who remained behind were employed by the sepoys for carrying away their own goods. As we were daily exposed to losses and maltreatment, we thought it would tend to our security if we employed two watchmen for the guardianship of the village. While these men remained among us, we continued free from visits from the sepoys; but, as we were unable to pay their wages, after a time we were obliged to discharge them. We then guarded the village ourselves, and saved it from the dacoits, who were plundering villages on all sides of us. One night, when the watch was being very carelessly kept, the village was entered by dacoits, who surrounded the house of Jud, and captured Benjamin, whom they beat very severely, to keep him from making a noise, and so waking up the other brethren. The Christians, however, gradually woke up and then fled into the jungles. In the meantime, the dacoits were beating poor Jud and pricking him with their swordsto compel him to divulge where he had hidden his money. After a time, he confessed that he had seven rupees in his clothes, pointing out to them where they were lying. While they went to search for the clothes, Jud seized the opportunity and fled. The dacoits, finding the money, departed, and the Christians presently returned to the village. The reason the Christians fled was that they imagined the Chakladar had come with his men to the village, and that, as he had commenced with the first house, which belonged to Jud, he would go through the whole village, house by house, beating the Christians. But this was a mistake.

"After this, we were constantly exposed to attacks from bands of marauders. Our clothes were torn off our backs, and whatever the vagabonds desired, they forcibly took from us. I will just give you an account of what occurred one Sunday. A zemindar, attended by several soldiers, came into the village. He asked us who we were, and on being told that we were Christians, said that the information had caused tears of blood to fall from his eyes, and that all of us ought to be killed. He then went to the house of Raphael, and seized some of the goods there, and wished to take away with him Grace, the mistress of the orphan girls. While the attention of this wicked man was engaged, this poor insulted woman ran from the house and took refuge in a field thickly planted with dal. Another Christian woman gave these wretches money to preserve her freedom. On the day following, the zemindar returned and surrounded the village with his men so that no Christian might escape. At that time I was seized, and they abused my wife with horrid language. The zemindar said that it would be better for us if we left the village, for if we did not, we should be killed. Our oxen and cows, that were feeding or ploughing, were taken away. Several of the brethren went with them. The cattle were given over to the commandant, and the brethren, whose names were Tobit, Obadiah, Frank, Newbolt, Sulaiman, Beson, and Timothy, were put into prison. On the earnest entreaty of these poor fellows, the commandant, who was a kind-hearted man, said he would try to obtain their freedom from the Chakladar. When the information about the Christians reached the Chakladar, he ordered that all the occupants of the village, men, women, and children, should be seized. The commander, who was perfectly helpless in the matter, was ordered off with a hundred men to Basharatpore. Obadiah accompanied the force. On seeing such a body of sepoys coming towards the village, we all began to fly into the jungle; but the sepoys, frightening us with their muskets, stopped us, saying they would kill us if we ran away. The commandant stated that he had only come to see that we had no European things among us. When the sepoys had searched every house and taken what they liked, the commandant gave the order that all the Christians were to be seized, agreeably to the Chakladar's instructions. Then Obadiah begged hard of the commandant, and said he would be security for the Christians, that they would all remain in the village. On this security, the commandant was prevailed on to let us remain where we were.

"On the evening of the day that these events had occurred, a Munshee, on horseback, came riding into the village. He said to us, 'You are very foolish to continue here; why did you not leave with the Europeans? and why do you not now leave a few at a time, and go to Bettiah? There is no certainty in this Nazim. He may order you to be killed, especially as the King of Delhi and the Nawab of Lucknow have commanded that all persons of the Nazaritish race should be put to death. When the morning came, the commandant went to the Chakladar and pleaded on behalf of the Christians, saying that no good would be gained by putting them to death. The Chakladar replied, Well, they must become Mohammedans. The commandant then came to the seven brethren who were in prison, and told them the orders of his master. The brethren said they would become Mohammedans, and on this condition were let off. The next morning, four of them returned to the commandant, who took them to the Nazim. This man abused them, and said, 'You are neither Hindoos nor Mussulmans; what kind of treatment shall I shew to you? The King has ordered that all Christians be banned from guns. If you become Mohammedans, you will save your lives.' The commandant then remarked that, 'If you make them Mussulmans, who will eat and drink with them? You had far better leave them as they are. To this, the Chakladar made no reply. The commandant hereupon suggested that the bullocks and cows taken from the Christians should be restored to them, and the Chakladar gave orders to this effect. After à great deal of difficulty, we managed to recover our cattle. The Lord saved us thus far, and did not suffer the enemy to kill us, as many were wishing to do. Before the above events took place, several of the Christians had left their families and started for Benares, much against the will of the rest.

"When the brethren who had been in captivity were set free, we all agreed that we had better not remain in the village any longer, but leave, a few at a time, for Shahpore, where we would all reassemble and take further counsel of one another. On the 12th October, Raphael died, and on the 13th, the brethren began to leave the village. On the 20th, I left with the orphan boys and girls. We all arrived quite safely at the appointed place of meeting. While in the village to which we had come, we were all thrown into alarm by the presence of a body of sepoys under the command of Musarraf Khan. Some money being collected for them, they were induced to leave. On the same evening, we took the road leading into the jungles. Two widows and an old man of our company wished to remain behind, and although we did all we could to induce them to alter their purpose, they would not do so. We were therefore obliged to leave them. Towards the evening of the day, we came to the village of Budhwar; on reaching which, what did we see coming to us in the distance? It was no other than the soldiers of the Chakladar. On approaching, they began to abuse us, and said-We have been following you with the greatest eagerness, and now we have got you; come along with us to the Chakladar. They then separated the men and, with their naked swords, ordered them to sit down there. Some of the sepoys went to our carts, and first of all seized all the swords they could find, and next our goods, cooking utensils, clothes, and so forth. When they had taken these things, they went up to the young men, who were standing apart, searched the clothes they had on, and took away whatever they found valuable. So they left us. During the whole night, we remained there, mourning over our loss. We could not eat, and could do nothing else but weep. In the course of the night, some sepoys belonging to the Rajah of Bettiah, who had charge of the neighbouring village, came to us. Through them, we obtained a few of our stolen things, and afterwards went to Shahpore, and remained there a day or two, consulting together what was best to be done.

"While at Shahpore, we saw a native Christian from Bettiah, and inquired of him whether there were any English gentlemen at Aligunj, Sewan. He stated that a magistrate and some Goorkhas were there, and that a body of European soldiers was expected in the place shortly. We continued at Shahpore for several days, and then started for Sewan, and reached Aligunj in four or five days. Mr. Lynch, the magistrate, shewed us great kindness and relieved our immediate wants. I feel much obliged to him for his attention to us all. The Rev. Dr. Ribbentrop visited us and had a religious service with us every day. After a time, the Rev. H. Stern arrived from Benares. We were all delighted at seeing him, and he at seeing us again. He took us to Chuprah, and provided us with clothes and other necessities, and made arrangements for our obtaining food twice in the day. He hired a house for us there, where we resided, some in the house, and some in a tent. Here we lived for a while. When Gorruckpore became cleared of the enemy, the Christians all returned, having obtained carts for the journey gratuitously, through the kindness of Mr. Macleod, the deputy-magistrate. On the tenth day after leaving, we arrived in Gorruckpore, thankful to our friends for their great kindness to us, and praying to God to grant them many blessings in return. Thanks be to God for all the mercies He has so graciously bestowed on us during the season of our weakness and distress! He has delivered us from great peril and brought us into a place of rest. We thought, when we were so heavily persecuted by the wicked people around us, our lives would one day be sacrificed; but blessed be the Lord, who has preserved our lives to the present moment, although several of the brethren lost their children both in Sewan and in Chuprah, yet. He did not leave us comfortless. Praise a thousand times be ascribed to our Protector, who has brought us safely back to our own city, which we had left weeping and sorrowful! I am quite sure that, as He has saved us from so many trials in the past, He will aid us in the future, so that we may serve Him with newness in life. The Lord grants us all strength that we may henceforth live as new creatures in Christ Jesus!"

Respecting the destruction of property in the Gorruckpore mission, Mr. Stern has given me the following statement. Writing from Gorruckpore, he remarks: "Our mission has suffered in all to the amount of about 10,000 rupees. All the out-houses are destroyed. The bungalows escaped with windows smashed, ceiling coverings taken away, and every article of furniture plundered. I picked up a few of my things, but not one book is forthcoming. The church is cleared out of every article, and even several graves, down to the mouldering remains of those that slept, have been dug up. The native Christian village at Basharatpore is, except five houses, entirely destroyed, all a heap of ruins. I hope we shall have another and a better village by and by. My native Christians have all returned. Schools are open, and services go on as usual."I trust the Church Mission will render liberal aid to our dear brother in his arduous work of re-establishing the mission at Gorruckpore. He should not be left alone there. The work is too heavy for one man to perform. The parent society zealously sends new missionaries to India every year. Might not one be spared for Gorruckpore?

Arrival of Bengalis in Basharatpur

According to the book of Dr. Ved Prakash Pandey, the arrival of Bengalis can be traced back to the arrival of European Indigo planters. They came here in search of food, shelter, and jobs. In the year 1802, some Bengali Muslims came to Gorakhpur and opened a hospital. The first civil surgeon to emerge was Dr. Muhammad Shah. He served here for 3 years, and the next doctor to serve here was Dr. Yogeshwar Rai. He served here for 20 years and retired. In 1847, Pran Krishna Ganguly arrived in Gorakhpur from Alambagh, Kolkata and later got involved in zamindari. He accepted Christianity here and received the power of attorney from the Anglican mission.

This account somehow relates to the statement of the account given in the book 'Shaharnama Gorakhpur'.

Some Bengalis came before the mutiny of 1857 for the business of woods and later became the owners of mission land after getting converted. The names mentioned are Kundu, Ganguly and Das. While talking to Sumit Ganguly, the descendant of the Ganguly family, denies these statements. He mentioned that his grandfather established the Ganguly tola and Garediya tola in Basharatpur. In addition to it, the The locality of Ashok Nagar was also established by the Ganguly family. In the same series, Ramnath Lahiri arrived in the year 1893 in order to work in the treasury office. His eldest son was Vishwanath Lahiri, the first I.P of UP police. The second son was Dr. KN Lahiri, who was a renowned medical practitioner of Gorakhpur. Likewise, Dr. Gopal Chander Ghosh Babu of Ghosh company Chauraha graduated from Kolkata University (previously known as London Mission College),who is the second master of the Anglo-Vernacular School and a successful homeopathic practitioner. In a picture of the CMS gleaner, Babu Chatterjee, a native convert of Bengal, was an English teacher in the Anglo-Vernacular School. Babu Durga, a native preacher in the mission, was also a convert of Bengal. In 1904, Aghor Nath Chattopadhyay became the principal of George School (Now Jubilee College). He was initially serving as a teacher in the school but was later promoted.

Co- mingling of Bengalis with christian community was very common as the railway first emerged from Calcutta, then covered the western parts of India.

Apart from this, a Bengali Hindu doctor, Dr. M.N Chakraborty, had done great work for the Swedish mission.

Zenana Bible and Medical Mission

On the last day of the year, we were called at 4 am to catch the early morning train to Gorakhpur. The journey of 160 miles occupied a little more than 12 hours, but we were pledged to spend New Year's Day there, and felt amply repaid for leaving the frequented main routes to come to this somewhat out-of-the-way place. It is an ideal Mission Station, and we were quite delighted with the work there.

Gorakhpur is a town of about 60,000 inhabitants, in the midst of a densely populated district bordering Nepal. The need for Mission workers in this district is very great. Gorakhpur and Basti are combined for administrative purposes, and in 1891 had 4,783,696 inhabitants. The Christian workers sent out by the Church to win this great multitude for Christ were at that time represented by one Missionary of the C.M.S. and two ladies who had just been appointed to work there by our Society! The Rev. H. Stern had laboured there nearly forty years and had charge of the congregations in the town and at the outlying Christian villages of Basharatpur and Sternpur. A native Pastor and a small staff of teachers and catechists were working with him. Our Society had 11 native teachers and Bible women. Let the reader imagine what would be the spiritual destitution of greater London if, to meet the needs of all its people, there were only two ministers of the Gospel, assisted by a few Scripture readers and Bible women, and he will realise somewhat of the need in the Gorakhpur district. The C.M.S. now has three Missionaries there, the Rev.

J. P. Ellwood, who is in charge, having long experience, and being thoroughly practical. Mrs. Ellwood is also the most energetic and able worker. One Missionary devotes his whole time to the large Boys' School; the third had just arrived and was learning the language. Gorakhpur is the headquarters of a Commissionership, and has several English Officials, and is also the chief centre of a railway, on which there are many European employees. As there is no other clergyman, the C.M.S. Missionaries contrive to hold two services in English on Sundays in addition to all the demands of the native Church. In connection with the Zenana work, we have six English and 21 native labourers, Miss Hibberd, who is in charge, having been there since 1892, and being highly respected.

New Year's Day was bright and busily occupied. It was given chiefly to the "Christian Mela" or Festival at Basharatpur, three miles off. The district suffered much during the Famine. The Missionaries helped many, but required them to earn the money. The women were taught needlework, etc., which was sold. The men were employed to dig wells of a sufficient depth to give water during the driest season, and to build strong walls inside them to prevent their falling in. Thus, the money given for Famine relief was utilized to provide against similar failures of crops in the future. The wells are in the middle of fields and will afford a constant supply of water for irrigating the crops. Lord Kinnaird was asked to open them, one being called after him. A short service was held at each. The crops were fresh and green, and the long strings of native Christians in their many bright coloured dresses looked very pretty as they wended their way from one field to another.

Girls school in sternpur

Then the Christians enjoyed themselves with games, running, climbing, &c. The scene was most picturesque, several gay flags adding to the variety of colour worn by the people. Nearly 100 boys from the Basharatpur Orphanage were present, saved from the Famine, and now looking well and strong. They were happy and thoroughly entered into the pastimes. But meanwhile, at the other side of the compound, a very different sight presented itself. A group of 34 poor, miserable, emaciated lads was lying about on the grass, or sitting helplessly leaning against a wall. They had been received the day before from a Government camp. Most of them were so weak that they could hardly walk. Some attempted to do so, but were too unsteady and gave it up. More than half of them had itching very badly. All presented the appearance of starvation and gross neglect. Yet it was two months after the Famine was supposed to be over, and they had been all that time in the Government Orphanage! If such a state of affairs had been found by a doctor in a Mission Orphanage, very strong measures would have been taken at once. Doubtless, Government Famine Funds had been fully drawn upon for these poor children, but how had the men to whom the money for their food was entrusted, and whose duty it was to look after them, escaped punishment? Fortunately for them, they had now come under Christian care.

The following day was Sunday, and a very busy one. The morning service for the native Christians was at 8.30. Mr. Ellwood baptized 30 boys and girls from the Gorakhpur Orphanages, all Famine waifs, but now looking well cared for and happy. Some had been picked up by our ladies beside the bodies of their dead mothers and were apparently beyond recovery. But kindness and care brought them round. At 11 o'clock, I preached at the English service, the collection being given to our Society. There were 58 present. In the afternoon there was a deeply interesting service at Basharatpur, during which there were 100 baptisms-viz., 18 men, 22 women, and 60 children, mostly from 5 to 12 years of age, It was delightful to see so many families coming out, and to feel that, although their profession of Christianity was cutting them off from many relations and friends, the home circles remained unbroken. They were poor people who had been cared for during the Famine and had been led to receive the teaching they then heard. The previous night, many of their relatives had come in to endeavour to dissuade them from disgracing their villages by becoming Christians! All stood firm, and now these heathen relations and friends were crowding the Church, and standing outside at the open windows and doorways, to watch the ceremony. It was the most solemn and interesting service. All the candidates for baptism were dressed in white, except a few boys from the Orphanage, who wore their dark coats. The Church, which holds about 400, was full to overflowing, and the many bright-coloured saris of the Christian women presented a most picturesque scene. The burst of response and the singing were very hearty. After the baptisms, the newly-appointed native Pastor preached a short sermon suitable to the occasion. There were a number of others who were being prepared for baptism, but were not yet ready. At the earnest request of Mr. Ellwood, we agreed to set Miss Hayward, one of our village evangelists, free for a year to continue the teaching of the newly-baptized women and children, and to prepare the others for baptism. She had had a good deal to do with them already, and they had given her a name which means "The loving one." Since then, in response to a further appeal from Mr. Ellwood, she has been lent to the C.M.S. for this work for another year. It is most important that poor people of this description should be carefully watched over during the early part of their Christian life and carefully instructed.

The evening service in English was at the Railway Institute. There was a large congregation, chiefly of railway officials, etc., to whom Lord Kinnaird gave an earnest, practical address.

Afterwards, we joined Mr. Ellwood's home circle, and according to custom, all the Missionaries in. The Station met and sang several hymns, closing with a reading and a prayer. The baptisms, of course, had been extra, but in. In other respects, this is a picture of an ordinary Sabbath at Gorakhpur, and would apply equally to many other Mission Stations. But the following day was also very fully occupied. In the morning, the girls from six Schools connected with our Zenana Mission were assembled in one large room for their Prize-giving. Upwards of 300 were present. They looked very pretty in their bright saris and wealth of jewels. Their ages varied from 5 to 10, but we were glad to find a number who were between 10 and 13. The singing was good, and also the recitations, especially of the Ten Commandments, and other portions of Scripture. The prizes, which were given away by Lady Kinnaird, afforded great delight to the children, especially the dolls!In the afternoon there was an open-air service, when Lord Kinnaird laid the foundation stone of a new Mission Hall, and afterwards we were invited to meet the European Officials and others at the Commissioner's, In the intervals we saw over the Boys' Orphanage, with the carpenters' shop, shoemakers' shop, and weaving sheds, in which they receive industrial training; and also the Girls' Orphanage, which is under the care of Mrs. Ellwood and is excellently managed. The work of the C.M.S. and of the Z.B. & M.M. here is closely connected that they can hardly be described separately. Mr. Ellwood said, "We are all one." Again and again, he expressed the very warmest thanks for the assistance which the ladies gave. During one of my visits, I stayed at the Zenana Mission House. It was a delight to be in such an atmosphere of earnest spirituality, faith, and prayer. Each morning, the native teachers and Bible women assembled for prayer before going to their duties. On Saturday morning, they have a special Scripture lesson, which is given by one of the

Missionaries as the groundwork of their teaching in the Zenanas, etc., during the following week. I was present at one of these lessons. There were 22 Bible women and teachers, 3 Zenana women who had recently been baptized, and 3 others who had just come out and were being prepared for baptism. All sat on the floor in the dining room, in a large semi-circle, with sheets of paper and pens in their hands, and took copious notes of the lesson which Miss Hibberd had prepared for them. In this way, the ladies ensure the teachers are kept up to the mark, and taking a regular course of Bible lessons, instead of getting into a rut and going over the same subjects continuously.

Ms. Hibberd teaching a Zenana

The ladies of our party had the pleasure of visiting one School from which the gentlemen were rigidly excluded, as it is held in a Zenana! The house belongs to a Brahmin, who invited Miss Hibberd to visit his wife to teach her. This she did for about three years, although the lady never appeared willing to receive Christian instruction. She was overjoyed at the relief from the monotony of her Zenana life which the visits of the Missionary afforded, and pleased to be taught secular subjects. But when her need of Salvation was spoken of, she would reply, "Is not my husband a Brahmin? He is a priest. If this were necessary, would he not tell me?" But God often uses sorrow to bring those whom he is calling to Himself. She had one little son, the only boy, and therefore greatly prized. This little boy became seriously ill. The priest tried charms and endeavoured to exorcise the evil spirit that is thought to cause illness, but in vain. A native teacher called and found the mother in great grief. She said, "We have tried everything, but it is of no use. There is nothing more we can do, and he is getting worse." The Christian teacher replied, "No; there is one thing you have not tried. You have not prayed to the Christian God. May I do so?" In her anxiety, the mother agreed, and the teacher prayed earnestly that the child might be spared. The prayer was heard, and from that time the little one began to recover. The mother says she has never prayed to an idol since. She is a true believer, and although unable to leave her Zenana and openly confess her faith in Christ by baptism, she witnesses Him in the midst of her own family. Soon afterwards, she was anxious to do something to bring others to know and love the Saviour. Her husband allowed her to gather a few little girls, daughters of other Brahmins living close at hand, and during the last two years, she has taught a little school regularly in her Zenana, in which she has about 30 pupils.

Mary Warburton Booth (Nurseries fellowship)

Mary Warburton Booth (1869–1955) was an English missionary and preacher whose ministry spanned over four decades, primarily in India, where she worked tirelessly to share the gospel and serve the poor. Born in 1869 in Leeds, England, she grew up in a Christian family and was educated at home by her parents, who instilled in her a deep faith. Initially uninterested in missionary work, she was profoundly impacted by her experiences ministering to the destitute in London's East End slums. In 1899, at age 30, she responded to a divine call to go to India, sailing there alone and settling in Bombay (now Mumbai), where she spent 35 years in service. Booth's preaching career began in India with the Church Missionary Society, where she focused on evangelizing women and children in villages across the Bombay Presidency.

She later came to Gorakhpur along with Ms. Powell to take charge of the Zenana mission. She opened an orphanage with the subscriptions sent by Capt. Dawson from England. The experience in this district was not good as she was forced to become a medical lady because of the terrible conditions of the children who were suffering from deadly diseases.

The nursery fellowship was running near the Gorakhpur University road, but was later handed over to the Himalayan Evangelical Mission.

Anecdote -

"How I wish I had known! I have lived in India for twenty years and have not yet seen one! Do, please, tell me when there is another and ask me to come! But I cannot wait; tell me about that one now," and because I am sure that you also want to see it, you can listen while I tell the Major's wife, as far as I can, how

It all happened.

It began with a letter-this is a copy :

Honoured Madam,

I beg to approach you on a certain subject. Having heard that you have in your beneficent care a young girl who is of marriageable age, I bring your most respectful presence the need of my son before, and if you think proper, I should deem it a great honour if you will answer by return. My son is in government service and earning rupees one hundred per month. He is a good Christian and a dutiful son. Whether you will agree to my request, I shall wait to see, and if you are willing, that my son and your girl should be joined together in holy matrimony I shall forever pray for the success and prosperity of your regal self:

Believe me, madam, Your most respectful, Mrs. AUGUSTA PAUL.

Reply sharp.

The following day, another letter :

Honoured and revered lady,

I place myself at your mercy. Your kindness has reached far. I am looking for a reply to my letter. I beg of you to study my case; my hopes are high that you will agree. If you ask respectable people hereabouts about my welfare, you will be informed.We have a house fields, and three bullocks. I have heard that your girl is of good caste, so she is suitable for my family. Will you kindly let me know if this is agreeable to you ~ A favourable answer will oblige.

You're obedient, etc.

I sat back and thought, and I am glad that there is a place where thoughts are heard. It is such a solemn thing to bring two people together, and when it may mean life issues, it is overwhelming-or it would be, if the responsibility were lightly taken or understood. "Heirs together of the grace of life "were the words that rang in my spirit.

"Would it be that? "I almost asked aloud. "Would Will Pujarwathe be happy? "I just sat back in the Secret Place of the Most High and waited for His Voice. It came, soft and low, like a cool breeze at evening, and so I talked with the child.

At first she seemed bewildered, and so surprised that no one asked for her . .. No, no, no I "h But we do not take the first answer as final. I told her to think about it, pray about it, and then give me her answer.

Now, Pujarwathe had never seen Augusta Paul, so she did not know what he was like, or if she would care for him. He told me that he had seen her "glorious visage "when he came out of church one Sunday. That was all, but it was enough to make me desire her! Saturday brought the prospective bridegroom, and he seemed very pleased and expectant as he entered the Bungalow, although there had not been time for an answer to the two letters.

He told me how he was a respectable Christian and a staunch teetotaller. He told me about his worldly possessions and then, lifting his hands, he said, "You see, madam, it is all as nothing when I have no wife."

I answered, "Let us pray! "And when we got up from our knees, the atmosphere was clear, and I said,"· I suppose you would like to see Pujarwathe and have a talk with her?"

"As you like," he answered.

And so I called her in and left them together.

But she was not going to talk to any man, so she stood perfectly silent in the middle of the room. He asked her questions, which she refused to answer, and then, having stood in the room with him for a few minutes, A fright seized her and she was gone. I saw her run across the compound, and I went back to him.

"She will not speak to me," he said, "she will not answer my questions, but that is all to the good; it is the custom of our country. I am willing to take her."

And being a woman, I answered, "I will see what ,he says," and then he went away.

A week later, he came again, but Pujarwathe refused to see him.

"Are you going to marry him?" I asked. "Just as you wish," she replied.

And that was all I got from her, but her manner showed that she was willing, and so I left her. Time gave her opportunity to think, and the following week she came shyly to me, saying that she did not want to marry, but as I seemed to wish it, she would go with the man.

I told her that it made no difference to me whether she married or not, except that I wanted her to be happy; he seemed a good man, and a real Christian. So, when he came again, he simply asked: "Is she Willing?" And I said, "Yes."

No, he did not want to see her to talk over anything; he was quite satisfied. And the date the betrothal was fixed for the following Friday.

There was great excitement in the family, for this was our first wedding; but the betrothal, which is a Public service, is a very solemn affair. About fifty guests were invited, and they all crammed into the Bungalow. When the Padre arrived, there was scarcely room for his feet; he had to stand in the doorway!

All the family and the guests were jammed together sitting on the floor, two chairs were put side by side near the Padre, facing the company, and on these sat the two to be betrothed; all eyes rested on them. Paul Augusta looked well pleased to be there, but Pujarwathe was shy and unaccustomed to the limelight. She sat with her head down, refusing to look up, And I sat next to her to give her courage! You see, our Pujarwathe was a child-widow, and she had suffered intensely when she was a Hindu. She bore the scars that pain makes, and although her life had been happy in Jesus for about three years, the scars were not effaced-she trembled at the publicity. The Padre stood, and having read a portion of Scripture relating to marriage, he turned to the two in the chairs. Addressing the man first, he reminded him of the why and wherefore of that meeting, reminding him also of the solemnity of the occasion, and then asked, "Have you anything to give as a sign that you wish to be betrothed to this girl - "

Then the would-be bridegroom stood up and said a few words about himself and his family, and his desire to be united with the girl present. Looking at her, he then handed two parcels to the Padre.

Tense excitement filled the air as he slowly took the wrappings from the parcel and revealed a crimson silk saree? No! A piece of flower-sprigged. material for a kurta? No! No! A silk handkerchief and a ring.

The company gasped and looked at each other in astonishment.

"Did you ever ?" their eyes said. "I never did," their eyes replied.

And feminine pleasure over the beautiful gifts ascended to its full height for all, apparently, except to Pujarwathe. She sat perfectly still, her head was not raised once during the service, and she took the gift as if in a dream.

"Pujarwathe, have you anything to give as a token that you are being betrothed to Augusta Paul? "Dead silence; all eyes were fixed on her. "Pujarwathe "-the Padre's voice was very tender and understanding. "Pujarwathe," he repeated,

"Have you anything to give as a token that you are willing to go with Paul Augusta? "But she sat there, her head downcast, and refused to answer.

I touched her arm, whispered to her, tried to push her forward to answer, but she was not going to let her voice be heard. After a tense silence that seemed like hours, and which was probably about sixty seconds, she turned her head away from him, and stretching out her hand, she gave the Padre a Bible and a handkerchief that she had brought for that Purpose! The gifts were all held up before the company and given to the man and woman. The Padre reminded them of the solemn promise, and after prayer, and he had blessed them, we all went into the garden to enjoy sweets and refreshments.

It was all over; as solemn and as binding as any marriage ceremony. Yet Pujarwathe had not uttered One word, but she had made her promise by her gift, and so the wedding day was fixed.

We stood outside and counted up the weeks, and then he said it should be the Wednesday after the third Sunday, as soon as possible after the banns were called in Church.

"Monday was not a good day. Tuesday was inauspicious-Wednesday would do; it was the best day and the middle of the week, so that was fixed with the Padre.

Arrangements?

Everybody was eager to help.

Pujarwathe took great interest in the preparation, and she made all her own trousseau.

Paul Augusta came to me to ask what he should send for her wedding dress-the bridegroom provides all the wedding garments, including footwear-

And when we had chosen a simple white saree, he went off rather disappointed, for he had thought of gorgeous apparel. But we believe that simplicity is the best,

and the bride, too, was very pleased.

The wedding was fixed for four o'clock in the Hindustani Church, but, as he spoke English and had been to France, he wanted to have a reception like those of the West, and it was to be in our compound! He said that he wanted "only to ask a few friends." That was all. They were to have tea and cake, a real bride's cake with white sugar, and then he would Take his bride home to his village, and they would have a great feast.

I took him at his word and said we would gladly have the reception here, as he only wanted to ask a "few "friends, and so we went forward.

The night before the wedding, the garments for the The bride arrived, all pure and white, as simple and as elegant as any wedding garments could be. When Pujarwathe was arrayed in them, she looked all a bride can look on that great day. A wreath of tuberoses held her saree in position, and an armful of flowers hid all her nervousness. Zorah and Stuttie, little three- year-olds, wore soft pink sarees and rosebuds, and walked on each side of her; then we started for Church. We arrived exactly at the hour fixed; the Church It was crowded. We were just about to enter-I saw some people coming up the path.

"He has not arrived yet," they said, and I sank back in the "Ford "with the bride.

"Shall we run away?" I said to her, jokingly.

She shook her head-" not willing "-but we drove off to view the landscape o'er while we waited for the bridegroom, and the strange thing to me was that no one seemed to mind or think it strange that the bride-The groom was late.

East is East, and it is futile to try to hurry it up.

It cannot be done. The only result to be attained is irritability and impatience. So we just wait and learn patience, and enjoy our drive.

When we got back to the Church, all was in order. The bridegroom, resplendent in a white silk suit, was waiting for us as we walked up the Church.

There are many ways of going to a wedding, and the Indians seem to know them all. Outside the Church was a medley of vehicles-a motor car, several tongas, tikke garies, ekkes, and bullock-carts-and when the service was over and we started back to the compound, it was a wonderful procession! But I never dreamt they were all coming to us. Yet, in less than an hour, over two hundred people arrived, and were clearing away all the cakes and sweets we had prepared for our family, and the "few" guests. While the children looked on in polite silence, I whispered to one, and it was carried round- "You shall have yours to-morrow" -and they were quite content.

Augusta Paul had his reception-the guests brought their invitation cards. I had one thrust into my hand :

MRS. PAUL AUGUSTA requests the pleasure of Mr. & Mrs. Din Dayel on the occasion of her son's marriage to Puiarwathe Singh. Reception in the Dawson Bungalow and Compound.

Date .... hour Tea and Refreshments.

Did you ever have someone invite over two hundred guests to partake of your provisions in your home and garden? And do it all in their own name too? It was a novel experience for us, but what could we do but smile?

There is no twilight here; it is light and dark-either one or the other!

The light disappeared suddenly, and the guests hurried off.

Paul Augusta came to me.

"May I take her home ? "he asked, and then he called for his garie.

In the meantime, she, knowing this would be, had been in her room preparing for the going, and when I called her, she dragged herself along.

The family crowded round the conveyance, all eager to see the last of her, but she just sobbed out her woe. "Tell her that I will be kind to her," he said to me.

And when I had assured her, she took her seat, and I beckoned him to sit beside her. His relations, seeing there was room, jumped in and filled up, and they drove off.

The last I heard of the bride was a loud wail and a big sob as the garie took them off to their village home.

Now, that does not mean that she is unhappily married. She wanted to tell us that she loved us, and that was her way-she would not hurt us by appearing to be glad to get away, so she howled out her love, and went gladly with her husband to his home, and like the stories of olden times, they lived happy ever afterwards.

She comes back and brings her bonny babies to be loved and admired, and she thinks that she is about the happiest woman in India.

And that is the story of her wedding.

Narratives of Ms. Ellwood

On leaving Sultanpur, I went by train to Faizabad (about one hour's journey), accompanied by Umra, who had come to Sultanpur for Christmas. We went third class and found. It is comfortable enough for a short journey. We had to change at Faizabad and Umra, and I had breakfast in the refreshment room and rested in the waiting-room for about two hours.

In the meantime, my servant had been making enquiries about the best way for me to get to the Lakarmandi Ghat, to enter Gorakhpore. He found we had to drive seven miles, cross two rivers by boat bridges, and the last two miles there was no proper road, only sand. Also, there was a danger of finding the bridges open and having to wait some time while boats passed through, and they could be joined up again. I came to the conclusion we had better start at once, so commandeered a tonga and an ekka for the luggage and said goodbye to Umra, whose train for Mussoorie did not go till later. I was lucky in having a very good horse and a man who did not shout at it the whole time, as is the habit of Tonga drivers. We found the bridges closed, so we did not have to wait, and succeeded in just catching the train, which left at 3 p.m. It was an interesting drive, as we passed through the very sacred town of Adjudhea, where there are several hundred Hindu Temples, mostly built along the banks of the river. This being the birthplace of Ram, who existed five to six hundred years B.C., it is looked upon as a great place for Pilgrims, and many millions of Hindu Devotees visit it yearly. Miss Fallon, of the Z.B.M.M., used to have a school and Zenana visiting here, but through lack of funds, the work was closed about 1908 and left to the Wesleyans, who are still working there.

I had a comfortable journey in a second-class carriage all to myself from Lakarmandi, and reached Gorakhpore at 8 p.m. Mr. Pelly, of the C.M.S., came to meet me at the station and asked if I felt equal to going to a dinner party at Miss Booth's bungalow, as he and Mrs. Pelly had been invited there to a Christmas entertainment. I was quite ready to go, and dressed as quickly as possible, and we were not very late. I was glad to see Miss Booth, Miss Page, and Miss Anning so soon. We had a delightful evening, and I arranged to come and see Miss Booth's work later.

Mrs. Pelly's chief work is visiting the Christian villages around Gorakhpore, so she knows all my twenty-two girls who are married to Christian men living in those villages. Consequently, it was better for me to stay with the Pellys than with Miss Booth-they kindly wrote and asked me to come before I left England.

Mrs. Pelly's father, Mr. Stern, was a C. M.S. missionary in Gorakhpore for many years, and one of the villages is called Sternpore after him. It is very interesting for her to be now in charge of visiting her father's work. I see much improvement since I was here four years ago-the people are all more friendly to each other. The next day, she drove me in her motor car to the principal village, Basharatpore, where most of my girls are living, and left me there for two hours and came again to fetch me.

I first went to Mohini's House. She has been married for about fourteen years, and has three girls and a small son, only a few months old. Her husband gets good pay, and she is the second teacher in the village Anglo-Vernacular Middle School, under Miss Dharmjit, B.A., daughter of the Indian clergyman who is in charge of the Christian villages. Mohini was sent to me by Miss Marston of the Z.B.M.M. (who was working in Lucknow) during the famine of 1897· She was one of the best and most satisfactory girls I ever had, and became a true Christian. Her influence for good in the school was incalculable, and from all reports, she seems to be the same now. She befriends all the younger girls from Sultanpur who have married and live in the same village. Her eldest daughter is going in for the Government examination this year, and although she is still very young, I was assured by Miss Dharmjit that she has every chance of passing sufficiently high to get a scholarship which will enable her to go on to a High School. (Since This was written. She has been sent to the Victoria High School at Agra and is doing especially well.)

MOHINI WILLIAMS,
Gorakhpur

Mohini's house was beautifully clean and tidy, and she promised to help me with a tea party in the verandah of Miss Dharmjit's house for all the girls,their husbands, and children living in the villages. We made out a list of all who might come, and there were about twenty-seven girls, husbands, and children, a hundred and thirty altogether- . Then we went on to another girl's house and saw her children, etc., and she came on with us to the next, who also joined the throng, until I had visited all in Basharatpore and had quite a big following. They all seem so happy and friendly together, which I think is partly Mrs. Pelly's doing. Last of all, we went to The Rev. Dharmjit's house and interviewed one of his daughters, who kindly undertook to arrange the tea on the next day but one at 4.30 p.m., which was the day I was leaving Gorakhpore.

The next day, Mrs. Pelly drove me to the other two villages, Dharmpore and Sternpore, where I saw more girls, and invited them to tea the next day. Dharmpore is called afterMr. Dharmjit's father, who was a great Christian worker about forty years ago in Gorakhpore under Mr. Stern, was Mrs. Pelly's father. We then went on to Sternpore and found only two Sultanpur girls living there, married to brothers of the same family. One seemed very happy and well-to-do, and proudly showed me some very fine twins of a few months old. The other

Ulfat, who lived in the same house with her mother-in-law, was not so happy.

I nearly always find that if girls are not happy after their mar-riages it is owing to their mothers-in-law, who think it is their right to manage them and their sons and everything to do with their household arrangements. Ulfat, who has always been a very delicate girl, threw her arms round my neck and said, "I cannot live here any longer; I would rather live in a poor house, only take me away from my mother-in-law." Her husband, who was present, put his arm round her and was evidently taking her part when the old mother-in-law appeared on the scene, and there was a great row. Ulfat seemed very afraid of her and clung to her husband, who did battle with his mother on her behalf.

He is evidently very fond of Ulfat and the two little boys she has given him. I could not do anything then, but asked them to come to tea the next day, and I would see if any different arrangements could be made.

Mrs. Pelly said the best plan would be to get some land for the husband in Basharatpore and let them live separately from the rest of the family, which was eventually done, and I believe they are happy now. Miss Booth has had almost the same experience with one of her girls, married and living in the same village.

In the afternoon, I went to call on Miss Booth, and Miss Page showed me all around their domain. It is wonderful how nearly all their funds are given in answer to prayer. Sometimes they seem to have no visible means of carrying on, and then the money comes from quite unexpected sources. They pray about everything, and all goes well.

SECOND TOUR IN INDIA

Miss Booth kindly promised to let me have her motor the The following day, to go to Basharatpore for the tea-party, as I did not like to use Mrs. Pelly's motor so much. She showed me her accounts, as she wanted me to see ·how justified she had been in giving up a good deal of the money which came to her through the Society, and trusting to faith and prayer to be able to carry on. A good deal more than half now comes in this way, and she has no fears for the future.

In the afternoon, I drove again to Basharatpore for the tea which Miss Dharmjit had provided in the verandah of her bungalow. It was delightful to see so many old girls and to meet all their husbands and children. We had a hymn and prayers, and I gave an address to finish up with. The girls gave me so many presents that I did not know how to carry them all away.

After dinner, Mr. Pelly drove me to the station and saw me off by the 8 p.m. train for Supaul, in the Bhagalpore District, where I was due to visit an old friend.

SUPAUL. BHAGALPORE DISTRICT

I had promised in the summer before going out to India to pay a visit to Mr. and Mrs. de la Motte Hervey, some friends who managed a sugar plantation in Supaul, but when I found it was such a long journey from Gorakhpore, the nearest Z.B.M.M. station, I had arranged to go I nearly gave up the idea. After all, I wanted to see them very much, and as there seemed to be plenty of time to get through all the different Z.B.M.M. stations before the Conference, I finally decided to go on.

The servant who was travelling round with me was quite excellent, and generally succeeded somehow in getting me a second-class ladies' carriage to myself, and looked after all the luggage and took the tickets, etc., and paid the coolies a most tiresome job, as they are never satisfied, and was altogether a treasure.

Starting at 8 p.m. from Gorakhpore, I travelled quite comfortably all night, and reached a junction, the name of which I forget, at 9 a.m., the next morning. There I had to change and wait three or four hours, but my friend had sent a servant with breakfast to meet me as she knew there was no refreshment room in the station.

After two more hours in the train, I arrived at Supaul at z. 30 p.m., and she and her husband came to meet me in a motor, and we drove over very rough sandy roads to their bungalow about two miles off.

They have a lovely bungalow with a very pretty garden right out in the wilds, and I had a most restful and enjoyable week staying with them. The Sugar mill was quite near, and I was taken all over it. The sugar cane is brought in from different parts of the district in bullock carts, and after being weighed and the cultivators paid, is put into a sort of long trough which is wound up by machinery into the mill. There, it goes through ten different processes of crushing and clarifying before the sugar is fit for sale in the bazaars all around. The present mill is to be given up soon, as two years ago the river changed its course for two miles (which is a way rivers seem to have in India) flooded the mill, and nearly spoiled thousands of rupees worth of sugar.

The· same thing will probably occur again and cause great loss to the proprietors, so they have decided to move.

We went for a long motor drive one day to see something of the country round, and bought some very pretty and extraordinarily cheap silk saris for me to take back to England, and perhaps wear if I speak at meetings. Mr. de la Motte Hervey's father was a Colonel and grandfather a General in India, and the latter had had a great deal to do with putting down the Thugs, and they lent me a book he had written all about it, which was very interesting and thrilling in parts.From Supaul, leaving about 11 a.m. I started back to Gorakhpore, arriving the next morning at 6 a.m. I went again to the Pellys and spent the day there, as I wanted to see Ulfat again and make sure that she was happy. I had tea, etc., at the station, and arrived at their bungalow just in time to prevent Mr. Pelly coming to meet me in the motor as they were expecting me at 8 a.m.

By coming to Gorakhpore that day, I unintentionally came in for a very interesting ceremony-the unveiling of the War Memorial to the Gurkhas killed in the Great War, by Sir William Birdwood, the Commander-in-Chief. It took place at 11 a.m. and the whole station was present. The bronze figure of the Gurkha soldier is placed on the Cenotaph I had already seen in the Academy of 1927 , and I liked it very much. Sir William Birdwood stood on the steps of the Memorial with all the Gurkha regiments drawn up in front, and after pulling a cord which unveiled the statue, etc., he gave a very fine address, first in English and then in Nepalese.

Afterwards, they all marched past, each regiment playing their different instruments. One regiment played

"Flowers of the Forest", and all ended up with "God save the King."

One part of the ground was given up to the relations of the Gurkha men and women dressed in marvellous costumes, who had come from Nepal for the occasion, and after the ceremony, Sir William Birdwood went up and talked to several of them. He finished his speech by saying, "The Great War was not the last War, but whenever the next war comes, we feel quite sure the Gurkhas will stand by us and fight as nobly as they did before, remembering their special motto-' It is better to die than to be a coward'."

After lunch, I drove again to Basharatpore while Mr. and Mrs. Pelly went to a Garden Party given by the Commissioner to the whole station in honour of the occasion.I found Ulfat much happier and living with her husband in a little house near Mr. and Miss Dharmjit, and quite a mile away from her dreaded mother-in-law. She was very pleased to see me, and all the other girls came running from their different houses when they heard I had come. They all seemed kind to Ulfat and told her to be sure to come to them if she was unhappy or wanted anything.

Where she lived before was quite a mile away from any of the other Sultanpur girls, but I am sure she will be quite all right now, especially as her husband is certainly a very good Christian man. It was nice having a peek at them all again.

That night-Thursday! left again at 8 p.m. on my way to Khurja, expecting to arrive at my destination at 8 p.m. on Saturday, but the train missed its connection in Lucknow, and the consequence was I did not arrive at Cawnpore till too late for the Khurja train, and had to wait there from 10.30 a.m. till6 p.m.

After all this turned out to be all for the best, as I was able to drive around and have another look at the girls I live in Cawnpore. I had a good breakfast at the station, and then started in a very shaky tonga. I was able to take one girl round with me to see all the others, and I had a delightful time. I got back to the station in time to have some dinner before the train started for Khurja. It was not a very restful night, as we arrived at 3·30 a.m., and were met by a servant sent by Miss Pearson with a note, saying it was impossible to meet me there in the night as the authorities had given orders owing to many robberies that have occurred lately, that no one must drive from Khurja Junction to Khurja City, about six miles, without an escort of police, and I had not let her know in time to arrange this. The consequence was I had to stay in the waiting room in the station till the train went on at ·7 a.m. It was bitterly cold, but I wrapped myself up in all my rugs and fur coat and sat in a long chair, and drank hot tea.

C.M.S Gleaner

GORUCKPORE, or Gorakhpur, has not yet been introduced to the readers of the GLEANER. It is a city of 51,000 souls, about 120 miles north of Benares, in North India, and is one of our old stations. The Society was invited to occupy in 1828 by Mr. Robert Bird, an official of the Indian Government who, with his sister, laboured most zealously for the good of the people. Miss Bird, in the midst of her usefulness, fell victim to cholera. In 1881, Lord William Bentinck, the excellent Governor-General of that day, gave the Mission a thousand acres of waste land, which was cleared and cultivated, and a cultural village built for the Native Christians, which was called Basharatpore, the "Town of Joy." It proved, however, to be in some respects a Town of Sorrow. More than one missionary was stricken down there by fever, and in the Mutiny of 1857,the village was destroyed by the Sepoy rebels. It was afterwards rebuilt and a new church opened, the pulpit of which was made out of wood intended by the mutineers to be used for gun-carriages.

In Goruckpore itself, and in the village of Basharatpore, there are 750 Native Christians. Some of the leading Nativist teachers are grouped in the accompanying picture, engraved from a photograph given to us by the Rev. Henry Stern, who has laboured at Goruckpore for nearly thirty years. The following notes, also kindly furnished by him, not only describe the men in the group, but incidentally reveal some of the various branches of work carried on in the Mission: — This sketch represents Borne of the Native agents of the Gorakhpur Church Mission, to whom the resident missionary is much indebted for the success of his labours.

Commencing with the upper row, the first on our right is Mr. Lockwood, a Eurasian, is in charge of the Boys' Orphanage, superintending in particular the industrial department. The second is Pundit Vidya Pot, whom I baptized at Basharatpur a few years ago, and who has since done good work, both as a preacher and as a teacher. The third (with the turban) is Masih Dyal, a Brahmin by caste, who was also baptized by me, and who is a fair preacher; but having been once a Fakir, and having led a roaming life in his boyhood, has been somewhat wanting in steadiness. The fourth is Samuel Mitthoo, who was brought up in the Secundra Orphanage, and was subsequently employed as a teacher in the Basti Mission School, where he did good service, and where he was in good report with Christians and non-Christians. He afterwards went to the Divinity School at Lahore, but returned after one year's study without completing his course, and is now engaged as a reader and teacher at Basharatpur.

In the second row, the first on our right is Babu Chatter-jeo, a Native convert of Ben- gal, who is an English teacher in the Anglo-Vernacular Mission School, in which he has laboured for several years with much success and much acceptance with his pupils, being of a very kind and conciliatory spirit. The one after him is Babu Patras, the senior catechist of the Mission, has- ing laboured there ever since 1853, with faithfulness and diligence. He remained with the Native

Christians at Basharatpur under the most trying during the Mutiny in 1857. He was originally an inmate of the Orphanage at Sigra, Benares, and was for many years also the able secretary of the Native Missionary Association at Gorakhpur. The next is the Rev. F.

- Secundra Abel, an orphan, of tho and subsequently the able head teacher of the same institution. Having distinguished himself as a successful preacher and teacher, he was ordained and was for several years Native Pastor in connection with the Church Mission at Meerut. He was, two years ago, removed to Gorakhpur, where he has given great satisfaction. He is a man of great abilities as a preacher and has also occupied much of his time in translations. The fourth in this second line is Benjamin Tobit, a native of Basharatpur. He was trained as a teacher in the Benares Normal School under Mr.

Treusch, and has since done excellent service as a teacher in the Anglo-Vernacular School at Gorakhpur, and acted also as head master of the Basti Mission School, the building of which he superintended with much ability and faithfulness. He is now a candidate for the ministry, and there is every reason to believe that he will, under God, become an able Native pastor. In the front row, the first on our right is Masih P Rakish, who is the son of catechist Patras, and who labours as a teacher in the Anglo-Vernacular School. He is an undergraduate of Calcutta University. Next comes Babu Durga Dey, a Native convert of Bengal, who, in connection with the

Gorakhpur Mission, has been labouring for many years as a bazaar-preacher, in which capacity he shows much ability and zeal, and is very acceptable to the public. The third is Phillip Obadiah, a Native of Basharatpur. He is an evangelist under the Native Missionary Association. The last is Baboo Gopal Chander Ghose, who, some ten years ago, was baptized by me at Gorakhpur. He is an undergraduate of Calcutta University, having received his education at Calcutta in the London Mission College. He has ever since been the second master of our Anglo-Vernacular School. He is a man of great ability, energy, and zeal, and the school is much indebted to him for its success. He is the same who took part in the discussion, as mentioned in the account of the late Visitation tour of the Bishop of Calcutta, who, after delivering a religious lecture, engaged in an interesting and lively discussion with several native gentlemen present (Gleaner, September, 1878).

Ghose Baboo is also well- known in Gorakhpur as a successful homoeopathist practitioner.

Assembly of God (AG Mission)

The Assemblies of God (AG) is a Pentecostal Christian movement that formally began in 1914 in Hot Springs, Arkansas. It was established by nearly three hundred ministers and lay believers who desired organizational unity during the period of intense spiritual revival in the early twentieth century. Rooted in the influence of the Azusa Street Revival, the denomination gradually grew into the largest Pentecostal body in the world. Its teachings emphasize evangelistic mission, baptism in the Holy Spirit, and belief in the second coming of Jesus Christ.

Within the Gorakhpur district of Uttar Pradesh, there has historically been only one Assemblies of God mission station. The Siswa Bazar station was initiated in June 1919 when Miss Annie Morrison, who had earlier assisted Miss Baugh and Miss Lee in Chapra, felt spiritually led to begin missionary work in the region. In the following year, she married Mr. J. H. Boyce, and together they continued the mission activities. During a later period when Mr. and Mrs. Boyce were on furlough, responsibility for the work was entrusted to Mr. and Mrs. L. M. Jacobs. Although their stay was brief, they reported several instances of villagers experiencing healing after prayer, which strengthened local interest in the mission's activities.

The mission work at Siswa Bazar initially combined evangelistic outreach with institutional services. A girls' orphanage was established in the early phase, which was later merged with the Assemblies of God orphanage at Bettiah. Similarly, a boys' orphanage that was started at Siswa Bazar was eventually integrated with the AG orphanage at Rupaidiha. Over time, the missionaries recognized the urgent need to focus more directly on spreading the Christian message among the large number of unevangelized people in the region. As a result, institutional activities were temporarily reduced to prioritize evangelism.

At that time, Siswa Bazar had a population of approximately six thousand people, while Maharajganj, an associated outstation, had around one thousand residents. In addition, hundreds of surrounding villages presented significant challenges as well as opportunities for missionary outreach. The total population of the Gorakhpur district during this period was estimated to be about 3.5 million. When the Assemblies of God mission began its work at Siswa Bazar, no other European missionary organizations were operating within a forty-mile radius. By the year 1937, however, the number of missionaries working in the area had increased to thirty-eight, including four from the Assemblies of God.

To effectively reach diverse sections of society, Brother Boyce appointed four male evangelists and four Bible women. They shared the Christian message among both higher and lower caste communities. Although many people showed interest and listened attentively, deep-rooted traditional religious beliefs often made conversion difficult. In 1935, the transfer of Miss Hacker's industrial school for young women from Basti to Siswa Bazar marked a significant development. With this move, Miss Sophie Erhardt and her team of Bible women also arrived, giving renewed momentum to the mission. Subsequently, a small church building was constructed, and a rented facility containing a preaching hall and a book room was opened, enabling wider outreach and greater engagement with the local population.

Paul Sharma further developed the church and school with the help of the World Evangelical Mission, and children from affluent families in the city also began to enroll for their education. However, Paul Sharma suddenly left for England for a short period. Afterward, Prem Kumar, a resident of Deoband, took over the management, and he continued in this role until 1971. In 1972, R.C. Sahu was appointed as the administrator, and he carried out several constructive works for this church, expanding the church's land to seven and a half acres. However, he passed away in 1997.

The church is now known as St. Andrews Church. Now this church is under the care of Y. Adam.

The current serving pastor over here is Yuhannan Adam. Missions Work in Siswa Bazar, Gorakhpur, India (Info taken from General Council Minutes)

1927 – Edith Dutton, Siswa Bazar Gorakhpur, India

1929 – James Henry Boyce Annie M. Boyce Siswa Bazar Gorakhpur, India

1931 - Sydney Bryant and Viola Bryant Siswa Bazar Gorakhpur, India

1939 – Sophie Erhardt Siswa Bazar Gorakhpur, India

Hattie Hacker Siswa Bazar Gorakhpur, India

Walter John and Minnie John, Siswa Bazar Gorakhpur, India

Citation - "Trailblazers of God by Dr. AC George"

Bharosa Ghar (American Pentecostal Mission)

On the 11th of November, 1911, that is the date of 11/11/11, a ship sailing on the river Saryu developed a technical snag, and its expedition had to be halted. The passengers decided to stop at a village nearby, called Bhagalpur, located in the eastern part of the United Province

(present-day Uttar Pradesh). From this ship disembarked an American lady in her mid-thirties, along with a small group of Indians belonging to the state of Gujarat. Soon the ship was fit to travel again, but the lady and her companions never embarked on it, deciding to stay in Bhagalpur for the rest of their lives.

The lady was Dorothy; she had married a man of Irish descent, but alas, her marriage failed at the turn of the 19th century. She grew up Christian and was aware of the teachings. Her failed marriage gave her a spiritual experience, and she decided to travel as a missionary to an alien country in the hopes of sharing it. She came in contact with the Mukti mission in Gujarat and created a congregation to be sailed to a place for spreading the gospel of God. In Bhagalpur, she, along with her companions, established the Bharosa Ghar Mission. The word 'Bharosa' means trust, and her aim through it was to establish faith and trust in the society she had adopted.

A church was established, and so were a school and an orphanage to propagate the idea of trust and love among the locals. Dorothy never advocated for a shift of faith among the people; rather she advocated for formal education, a foreign concept for the villagers The mission she established still flourishes today and works for the welfare of the locals. It is a tribute to a lonely woman away from her homeland more than 100 years ago, with a strong commitment and aim. And Dorothy toiled for it till her death in 1946. After her death, Munshi ji (Samuel Morar) looked after the mission. A few years before her death, she had adopted three children from the orphanage; they were later honored with her name as an effort towards the continuation of her legacy. She named her adoptive son Prem, which means "love. It signifies the mature love that was the moving force in Dorothy's life.

It is fascinating that a woman in that era was enigmatic enough to convince people to follow her-as women who assume leadership still face backlash today. Dorothy was a strong woman.

Her strong morals were her guide, and through her, the village of Bhagalpur experienced the dawn of its betterment. Her story is inspiring. It is an example of how our lives introduce us to our destinies. Had her ship not broken down that fortunate day, and although she must've thought it to be unfortunate, she would have never realized her aim in life. Perhaps the fulfillment that she had hoped to achieve from traveling to India would have never been hers if her ship hadn't broken down that day. She could've gone anywhere, but she decided to settle for a primitive village. She found potential in Bhagalpur, and so she stayed on. And this stay forever changed the trajectory of growth for this village. The change she brought was in a small village, but the impact she had was big, and it was felt throughout generations. She devoted her life to what she believed was good.

The discovery of Dorothy was made throughout my life, through my father and his family. The discovery was that Dorothy Louisa McCarty was the foster mother of my grandfather. The discovery was the comfort of knowing that the woman whose name I carry was no ordinary one. And so the discovery of the woman named Dorothy continues

FOUNDER - SIS. DOROTHY McCARTY

CO-FOUNDERS : PASTOR & SIS. SAMUEL MORAR

Salvation Army

The Salvation Army was a Christian missionary set up by William and Catherine Booth.

This Mission started its preaching by opening settlements for the criminal tribes (Doms). Fredrick Booth-Tucker, an assistant Commissioner and the son-in-law of Mr. William and Catherine, was supervising the Mission.

These settlements were opened near the old police lines but were shut down in 1919 as his wife went back to England owing to bad health

Mission Itinerary Tours.

Knowles, S Missionary To Gonda

Friday, the 6th, found us in MaharajGanj, camped in as fine and noble a park of trees, surrounded by fields of wheat and barley ripening to the harvest, as could be found in any part of the world. The brethren had been at work on the road, and brought in a young Brahman, whose mind had been enlightened and his heart persuaded by the Gospel words of love preached to him. We all met in our tent, and after Dr. Johnson and I had further instructed and prayed with him, we baptized him on his confessing Christ with his mouth, and changed his name from Shri-Rám to Shri-Masih. His age is about nineteen, and his village is Shankar Nagar, a few miles to the north of Balrampur. Brother McArthur was asked how long this new disciple of Christ had been under instruction, when he answered: "For five miles!" Five miles of instruction is not bad for any man. A Satnami faqir (a religious mendicant of "The True Name," who is supposed to have broken away from idolatry) was also touched by the Word spoken to him in this place, and said he accepted Christ as his Saviour. We had another meeting in the tent, and after much instruction and earnest prayer, we baptized him under the name of Gukha'i and gave him the prashad, a piece of the unleavened bread that is divided among us when one is baptized; as a sign of fellowship. He remained some time with the brethren, and then went to his village. The bearer of the P. W. D. bungalow near, and another fakir, were so impressed by the Gospel preached that,though they were not baptized, they both said they believed in Christ, and would pray to God henceforth in his name. A middle-aged man, who had been an immigrant for fourteen years in one of the West Indian islands, came with two very interesting children, and said it would give him some em-ployment he would gradually break away from his estate and become a Christian. We instructed and prayed with him for a long time, but though his mind had received the light, he could not submit his will to Christ and seek first the kingdom of God. He seemed to be afraid that after we baptized him, we would turn him out and despise him. He said he believed in his heart, but left us without being baptized. It was rather late in the evening when we met for prayer again and went forth to a village adjoining our resting-place. By the best of drum we gathered and seated about fifty persons, and began our usual services. Three men were undoubtedly genuinely affected by the Gospel they heard; and one man made a move to come forward, but his wife, who, with other women, had been listening some little distance off, cried out to come home, and so he was kept from his good purpose. At that moment, a flash of lightning, followed by a loud clap of thunder, warned us of the storm that had slowly gathered up from the western horizon. and would soon deluge our camp; so we had to hasten back for shelter to our tents.

In the itinerary tours, we pitched our first camp at Maharajganj 15miles away from Balrampur .After our usual preparatory services in the afternoon, with united faith, we marched to the front of the shop of a vendor of spirituous liquors, situated at the head of the village. The expressive sign of this reeking, foul-smelling The shop was a long pole with a broken bottle hanging by the neck. It is very significant that the word the native uses to express intoxicating drink, viz. dárú, is the same he uses for gunpowder, thus dárú-sísá (lit.) powder and lead, means ammunition. And truly, as far as the effects go, the one is about as dangerous and destructive as the other. We found about twenty men and women sitting on one side of the shop, drinking and quarrelling together. And as far as we could judge, there was not a sober person among them. Of course, they were of the korí caste, the tribe our sáís or groom comes from, and I must say that during my long experience in Oudh I have never seen a respectable native of high caste drinking at these shops. We soon collected over a hun- Dred persons. After our customary service of song and prayer and preaching, we gave our invitation for any impressed to come forward and acknowledge it. The kalwár, or liquor The vendor himself was the first to respond to our call. He promised he would give up his questionable trade; worship God in and through the name of Jesus Christ; and as far as he knew it, always walking in the way of truth. On this confession We baptized him. He has since separated himself from the liquor business and gone back to his village to cultivate his land. When we had baptized this liquor dealer, his poor wife came running out to us saying that, "áp ne merepurakh kí zát ko bharisht kiya," i.e "You have polluted My husband's caste! "We told her only sin, as drunkenness, etc., could pollute and debase; and that we had raised her husband's caste by making him a Christian. After we had received the kalwár and pacified his angry wife, a poor blind man cried out: "These men speak the truth, and from this day I am also a disciple of Jesus Christ." With his sightless eye-balls turned to the setting sun, we received him as a chelá or disciple of the Lord Jesus Christ.

We too baptized some natives of Gorakhpur who had come to Gonda to meet us.

German Mission Zeimann of Ghazipore

1. The sun Eclipse Melá at Bullia was visited by me and Mr. Lorbeer on the 18th August, Mr. and Mrs. Howe were very kind to shelter us in their house and entertained us most hospitably; here many thousands of Hindoos came to bathe during the Eclipse in the place where the Sargoo falls iuto the Gauges; we preached to them the way of Salvation and forgiveness of their sins in our Lord and Saviour Jesus Christ; they were quite astonished to find us also there. One Zamindar Brahman said, "Have you come here also? Wherever we may have a Melá in honor of our Deotás. you follow us and make our minds uneasy."
2. The Kartik Melá at Bullia from 24th October to 4th November, here not less than 2 láks of people assemble, not only to bathe in the Sargoo and Ganges and worship Brigmuni, but especially for trade. I and our Catechist were joined as usual by the Rev. Mr. Heinig and his Catechist of Benares and our Cate-chist of Buxar and we preached for 5 days from morning till even-ing by turns to crowds of attentive hearers, formerly we had our place under an old pakar tree, this however was blown down lately by a heavy storm; but as this place is a very convenient spot which all the people have

to pass, Mr. Howe and Capt. O. Donda very kindly procured for us a Shamiana, by which we were greatly protected from the burning of the sun, and of which people also took advantage to stop by crowds and hear the preaching of the Gospel. The greatest care of the authority is taken to make the people comfortable.

3. A Mission tour was undertaken by me from the 11th November till the 25th January, in which I was accompanied by our Catechist, Anand Masih, of which I hope a few remarks from my Diary will be interesting. "The 11th November as far as Badipore, preached on the way in several places to attentive hearers; the 12th Chiraya Koth a Police Station, a large attentive congregation, the 13th Azeemgurh, comfortable entertainment with the Rev. Mr. Mallet, at the same day a large attentive congregation on the Bazár, and likewise on the 14th; on the 15th Sunday, I took part of the Holy Communion, and in the evening I was allowed to preach in Mr. Mallet's Church, on the 16th I visited a large Bazár at Azmagurh in the District, where I had a large attentive congre-gation, afterwards I was called to the house of the rich Baboo Beni Prasad, and had a long conversation with his son and others. An immense assembly was present, and I hope that many have left with good impressions. I gave them some tracts, and the young Baboo purchased the New Testament. Baboo is allowed to

keep Sepoys to protect his Treasury, which consists of 24 lakhs of Rupees. This privilege is for the services which he rendered to the Government in the mutiny. In the evening, I was very kindly entertained by the Collector who was encamped there, the 17th Dohri Ghát, an attentive congregation, the 18th Barhall, Great Bazar, a large congregation, and quiet hearers. The 19th Kouri Ram, preached to attentive people; the 20th Goruckpore, kind entertainment with the Rev.Mr. Stern, the same day, a large and remarkably quiet congregation in the Bazár; the 21st ditto, the 22nd Sunday, I was allowed to preach to the native Christian congregation in the Basharatpore Church and to partake of the Holy Com-munion and in the afternoon preached in the Goruckpore Church and departed on the 23rd to Khalalabad, a Police Station, large congregation in the Bazár, and in the evening at my tent a religious conversation with the Tahsildar and other native officials. On the following day I passed Maghar; here are two tombs of the Guru Kabir, each within a separate compound, of one a Mahometan has the charge, and of the other a Hindoo Fakir, both are disciples of the Kabir, and each of them asserts that the Kabir is buried in that tomb of which he has the charge and denies and opposes the other; this is a chief pilgrim place of all the disciples of the Kabir, who number 50,000, it is said, over the country: they come and worship there and offer in January on each tomb, in the hope that if the Ka bir be not buried in the one, he may be in the other, and in this way each of the Fakirs obtains so much offerings, that he can live comfortably. In the village, there are many of the Kabir disciples, they always acknowledge our Religion as the true one, their Righteousness in which they trust, is that they do not worship any idol or Hindu gods and not eat any meat. The 24th Basti, kind entertainment with Mr. Cooke, preached two days in the Bazár to attentive assemblies, the 26th Rodouly, preached in the Bazár to quiet hearers, and was called to the Zamindar and had a large congregation at his door, all heard the preaching of the Gospel in quiet attention; the Zamindar told me, that he was a great friend of Sarkar Angrez, and that he shewed great bravery in the mutiny, when a gang of rebels were sent by the Rajah of Athrouly, to rob his property; he and his friends got up to his two storied house, and defended themselves against the rebels, shot 7 of them and the rest run away without any success, for this his bravery he received a great many of villages as a Grant from Government, and is now able to keep an Elephant which he could not before. I gave him some tracts and the New Testament, and told him that for the latter, I would take 4 annas from him though it was much more worth, he promised me to send the money to my tent, I was however surprised when in the evening he returned the Testament, not willing to pay anything for it, kept however the Tracts. I was much struck when I was preaching on the Bustee Bazar, and a poor man appeared before me and complained, saying, "The Zemindar at Rodouly murdered my brother two years ago, but as he is Khair Khwah to Sarkar Angrez, we could do nothing to have him punished for his deed. The 27th Bássi, a very civil and religious conversation with the Rajáh, and preached in several places in the city to attentive hearers." The 28th reached Matehenua the estate of Mr. Peppin, here was a large Bazar; on going there, some Hindoos accompanied me, before we reached the Bazar, my companions pointed to the left at some thorn-bushes saying, there lives a Willaiti Sahib, who has become a Hindoo Saint, worshipper of Mahadeo, Mr. Peppin has built for him in the bush a little house to live in.

Curiosity made me to enquire more about it, as I thought it was not the fact, they how-ever insisted upon, that it was so, and persuaded me to go and see him, but at first I should report myself to his disciple, a young Brahman, who had received education in the Futtehgurh Mission School, named Budsyn, he lived in a separate small house; I went to the disciple who told me that Capt. R. was the Hindoo Saint, who sometimes called himself Mahadeo and sometimes said he was Jesus Christ himself. The Brahman n fantastic man, reported to me to him, and requested permission for me to visit him; he returned, however, saying, C. R. would not permit any European, even not Mr. Peppin, to see his face. I could however not abstain from being myself convinced, whether this Hindu Saint was a European, therefore I took courage to go and see him, his disciple and Anand Masih and my Cooly followed me; his door was open, and to my astonishment, I found a real European in him, almost naked, of a fair complexion, blue eyes, light hair, about 35 years of age, walking up and down in his little room. Seeing me he made sign to go away without speaking, I greeted him friendly, when he saw me still standing, he pointed to a paper fixed on the wall in his room to read that; the contents of that written paper were "that every one was forbidden to enter the room and begin any conversation with him; should however any one do so, it would be of evil consequence." I could, however, not abstain from speaking a few words to him about my object of coming there and that I was preaching the Gospel of our Lord Jesus Christ to the poor heathen. At once, he began to speak and pointed to his disciple, telling me, "This is Judas Iscariot, who betrayed his master; he never will be forgiven." his meaning was, his disciple ought not to have allowed me to come and see him. Then he advised me to adopt his dress; I replied that our Saviour had given no Commandment in what kind of dress His Gospel should be proclaimed. On this, he made a sign to leave him, and told his disciple also to go, and never to come before him. Much I heard afterwards about him; whenever the natives go of curiosity to see him, he spits them in the face, and orders his disciple to do it, for this reason no one will go near him; he is of great offence to the natives, and from several Europeans I heard afterwards, that if Government would send him to Europe, great offence would be removed out of India. I had a very large attentive congregation on the Bazar, the 29th Sunday, kind entertainment with Mr. Bridgeman at Newra, conversation, and several books sold to his servants. From here I marched to Balrámpore, and passed through Alidepore, Chillia Misri, Kathela.

Mr. MacGibbon's estate, Etwa Police Station, Biskohar, a large Mahajan's place, Pipra and Abar, in each place, I had a good opportunity to preach the gospel to a considerable and attentive congregation, who generally confessed that never any Padri had been there; they purchased books with great desire. In Pipra, some Opium cultivators came and expressed their great delight in seeing me in their village, saying that they had heard me preaching to them and other opium Assamies at Ghazeepore; they brought a

Chárpáe, spread cloths on it for me to sit on, brought me nice milk, and asked for any service they could do me. A great assembly soon surrounded me to hear the word of salvation: Balrampore, I reached on the 4th December, the Maharajah was not at home but stayed as a Member of Council in Calcutta. I had, however, an interesting audience with his old Hindoo Dewán; he expressed that his opinion was that any Religion man might be in was good; a respectable Mahometan being present in the assembly told him that the Padri Sábib only understood the Christian religion as the right one and only Jesus Christ the only Saviour for all mankind. Oh! replied he, if that is the case, then Jesus Christ will himself reveal to him whom he wishes to be saved; why then do the Padri Sáhibs trouble so much about others' salvation! He, as well as others of the assembly, took books with pleasure. On the Bazár I had a large crowd of attentive hearers for a long time, at once a young Mahometan rushed through the crowd, standing before me saying in the Gospel of Matthew is written, that Jesus Christ said to his disciples, that Mahomed would come after him and every one ought to obey and follow him; when he was convinced of his error, he went away quietly; from here I proceeded to Baraitsh, passing through Ekouna and Tillaq-pore where I preached in four places to attentive hearers and reach-ed Baraitsh on the 7th and was very thankful to enjoy here the kind hospitality of Mr. and Mrs. Chapman. As soon as I came to the Bazár, a respectable Mahometan merchant rose from his shop, greeting me with great civility saying, Oh Sahib, how glad I am to see you here again, since 4 years you have not been here to preach, stop here and take your place here in front of my shop, plenty of people will assemble to hear you, he brought me a chair to sit on, I was greatly cheered and encouraged by this man and told him, that I always use to stand and preach; so I stood onhis shop stair; very soon 1 had an immense crowd of Hindoos and Mahometans before me, who heard my address with best attention; young Mahometan appeared also before me having the Gospel of Luke in his hand, after he had heard me for a long while, then he asked me with great respect, to allow him few questions to me, which of course I did allow him; his question was as usual of all the Mahometans, viz. "You always say that the Lord Jesus Christ is the son of God, but here I have the Gospel of Luke in whose first chapter the birth of Jesus is pronounced, but nothing is said about the son of God." I told him to open the Book and read from the 20th till the 35th verse; here the Lion was shared in his own den. Convinced of his error, he left very quietly the crowd, who heard with great civility my preaching till in the dark evening. The following day,

I had the same interesting hours. Baraitsh is known by the Mahometans and Hindus as a famous pilgrim place on account of the tomb of a Mahometan named Sayad Salár, who came some time ago, with a gang of armed Mahometans from northwest, with the intention to fulfill the Koran, by killing all the Idolaters as Hindus in that part of the country who refused to become Mahometans; the Hindoos however who did not like to become Mahometans, opposed them; Sayad Salár was killed and his companions dispensed; now Sayad Salár is called a famous martyr, his tomb is worshiped by high and low Mahometans and Hindoos, and rich offerings are presented, of which the Maho-metan Fakirs make use; besides his tomb a tank is made, by bathing in it is pretended by these Fakirs, every year at the great Mela, two blind receive their sight; when I alluded to this pretend-ed miracle before the people on the Bazár, the Mahometans them-selves proclaimed, that it was all lie, never any blind had received his sight. From here, I proceeded to Gondah, at Piágpore, I had the pleasure to join Capt. Mainard and Lord Nonford at dinner, who were encamped there; on the 10th, I reached Gondah, after I had preached in several places on my way, I was kindly entertained by Major Ross and Mrs.

Caveneugh; on the Bazar I had a very large and remarkable attentive congregation; from here I marched on to Fyzabad. On the 11th, I visited a Mela at Balesar in the interior, where the Brahmans and others were very civil and attentive, and took many tracts and books. This Mela was never visited before by any Missionary; on the 12th Wazeerganj, remain-ed at night, the following day being Sunday, I left my tent under the Mangoe trees, and proceeded to the interior, to go with Anand Masih to his village Gohani, on our way, we had to pass through Rámpore the residence of the great Taalluqdar Kishadutt; he was not at home, but in his palace we had an interesting audience with his nephew and his Brahmans and officials, all were very civil and attentive to my address, and took books with great pleasure and desire. In Gohani, the inhabitants received us with the best civility, and I was permitted to have a visit and religious conversation with Anand Masih's wife, who was still a bigoted Hindoo Brahmani, and never joined her husband since his baptism on the 7th August 1864. She had already so far that she permitted Anand Masih to marry any other, saying, "I am a widow since you have become a Christian and shall remain a widow as long as I live." My conversation with her turned out most miraculous to the great surprise of all. She said, "very well, from hence I shall join the Pandit, my husband, and go with him, to remain with you at Ghazeepore to be more instructed and become also a Christian."

Anand Masih was so filled with joy that he asked me to come with him to a separate room to offer thanks for the great things the Lord had done that day, which he hardly expected before. I promised her to send her husband back from Fyzabad, to get a cart for her to bring her to Ghazeepore. After I had preached more to the residents, we returned to our tent; on our way however, we took advantage of preaching to a large congregation on the public Bazár at Rámpore; the 14th we visited the most important corn market at Nawabganj close to the Gogra; there I had in several places large attentive

congre-gations and sold as many copies of Scriptures, as I had with me, and gave away many tracts. At Fyzabad, I had the pleasure to enjoy the very kind invitation of Major Smith, and had a large congregation on the bazár to preach to; on the 7th, I went on to Lucknow; on my way, I had a large congregation at the important Bazár of Camierganj, the people were very civil. Anand Masib, I had sent back from Fyzabad to bring his wife to Ghazeepore, according to my promise; on the 19th, 1 reached Nawabganj Barah-banky, had a very large attentive congregation on the Bazár, and spent an interesting and blessed Sunday with Messrs. Luard and Gote, and Major Chamier and Col. Lewis. On the 21st, I arrived in Lucknow and was favored with a very convenient and comfortablelodging and hospitality by Mr. and Mrs. Hannah; the latter being a Pastor's daughter of Pomerania, had invited me long before. I made a stay at Lucknow, till the 30th December, and enjoyed the kindness of many Christian friends. The Reverend Chaplain, B. Morrell, M. A., who was formerly here at Ghazeepore, gave me very kindly a note of introduction and recommendation to solicit the Christian residents, kindly to assist me with their liberal contribution towards this Mission. It was of great blessing to me to find here so many christian friends in the military and among the civilians. Several officers take a warm interest in preaching and edifying their Christian fellowmen, as Captain Currie and Captain Morton preached in the evening in the Mission Chapel to a considerable congregation; even so, several preach in the Soldiers' Chapel, in which I also was allowed to speak a few words to the pious Soldiers. Captain Pasley has a prayer meeting in his house, at-tended by a considerable congregation of military officers and others; besides this, he is most anxious to infuse some spiritual nourishment into the native christian drummers of his Regt., to whom he gives lectures and prays with them on Sundays; during my stay there, he allowed me to do it. I do not doubt that much good towards many immortal souls is done by these pious and godly people. During my stay at Lucknow, I received a letter from Major Orr, at Roy Bareilly, who wished to see me and to request of me a Catechist to disseminate the Glorious Gospel in his 12 villages, which he got as a grant from the Government, for his good services which he rendered during the mutiny.

Hence, I left Lucknow on the 31st, with hearty thanks for all the blessings which I had received during my stay at this place, and proceeded now to Roy Bareilly. At Mohanganj, I saw a splendid, expensive new Hindu Temple, built by Raja Káshiprashád. I was told that at the consecration of this heathen temple, several Europeans who were invited by the Raja were present; many Hindu Temples have been erected in Oudh since the mutiny. In the afternoon, I had an interesting meeting with the Rev. Mr. Wilson, who was in camp with his family and on their way from Roy Bareilly to join the Annual Missionary Conference at Bans Bareilly, we both visited a public Bazár and had a very attentive congregation. At Rai Bareilly, I arrived on the 2nd January 1869; Major Orr's Bungalow I found empty, both the gentleman and Lady were encamped (16) ed in the village Rámpore in the district on the Bank of the Ganges, 4 cos distance from Fattehpore, to which place they invited me by a letter. During my stay at Roy Bareilly, I was most kindly treatedentertained by Col. and Mrs. Steel. My preaching was here on the

Largo Bazár at Moonshiganj; on the 4th, I marched on to Rámpore, and passed through Lalgunj, in which Bazár I preached in several places, and had very quiet attendants, and on the 5th I reached Rampore, where I was most civilly received and entertained by Major and Mrs. Orr; we agreed that Anand Masih should become their Catechist, after his wife would have been baptized. There I also met Capt. and Mr. Clifford, Brothers of Mrs. Orr, who stayed with them a few days for a short visit, and shot 8 Leel, who were very injurious to the field, one of them killed a few days before, a poor native who wanted to drive him from his field. On the 7th I left for Futtehpore; Major Orr was very kind to assist me with 4 Bullocks to pull my cart through the deep sand to the Boat on the Ganges; after I had crossed, I found a great deal of sand also on the other side, through which my two Bullocks pulled with great difficulty. An influential Brahman of the village, seeing my difficulty, came immediately with some strong people to lay hands on me and did not leave me until they had assisted me to bring the cart through the whole sand. I thanked them and spoke a few words to them and gave them some tracts, for which they were very glad and made their Salám. On the 7th, I reached Futtehpore, and had the great pleasure to enjoy the kind entertainment of Mr. Carnac and Capt. Young. Now the large Mela at Allahabad was beginning, which to visit, I had from the beginning of my tour intended; hitherto I had done my whole tour walking, which aggregated to 278 miles, to reach the Mela in time, I preferred therefore to go at once by Rail, and ordered my Bullock cart to follow after; hence I arrived on Saturday evening the 9th Janu-ary at Allahabad, it was half past 10 o'Clock, when I found most convenient quarter and entertainment with my old friend the Rev. Mr. Walsh, in which house I enjoyed during my stay many blessings; the following day on Sunday, he allowed me to preach in his Church, to his native Christian Congregation, and the following day he took me down to the Mela, where he already as usual had pitched a convenient tent, in which to preach to the thousands of by-passers of the pilgrims. I found my old friend and MissionaryBrother Heinig of Benares and some Catechists already engaged, but all were very glad and kind to allow me also a place and turn to preach. I was very fortunate to enjoy this privilege for 4 days when the Mela was well attended, and the heathens heard very attentively; the Missionaries of the Church of England and Baptist Missionaries had also, at some distance, their tents and preaching places. I felt very happy for all the blessings which I enjoyed at Allahabad with so many Christian friends and to disseminate the Glorious Gospel to so many benighted Hindu Pilgrims. May the Lord bless all our feeble efforts for the salvation of many immortal souls. In the meanwhile I received letters from my Missionary Brother Lorbeer, to finish now my Mission tour and come and join them again in the Mission work at Ghazeepore, for which I also longed. I left therefore on the 19th Allahabad, and arrived at Ghazeepore, thank God, in safety and good health, and was very glad to find all so well, and that Mr. and Mrs. Lorbeer had carried on the Mission work during my absence to the best satisfaction; Mr. Lorbeer performed, besides teaching the two highest Classes in the School, the Divine Services in our Native Christian Congregation and all other Mission affairs.

4. In the middle of February, I visited the Shivratri Mela at Berhampore in the Arrah District, where I was assisted by Mr. Gaustad and his Catechist of Buxar; there we had full work for 2 days, thank God, to crowds of attentive hearers.

In conclusion we desire to remark that Major Orr, afterwards requested us for another Catechist with the kind offer, that he would willingly support them both, to which we also agreed; hence on the 1st of June last, Anand Masih with wife, and Benja-min with wife and child departed from here and have arrived there at Roy Bareilly to the great satisfaction of Major and Mrs. Orr.

Anand Masih's wife was baptized here together with 11 others on the 9th May and was admitted to the Holy Communion on Pentecost. The motive and desire for the conversion of the benighted heathen subjects of Major and Mrs. Orr is most gratifying and cannot be valued enough; may the Lord bless now the efforts and labor of these two Catechists and make them instruments for the conversion and salvation of many of their benighted heathen countrymen to the Glory of His Holy Name. Amen.

We must not omit to mention the beggars who have generally received grain at the gate of our compound on Friday, and the Gospel preached to them; they numbered about 200. Since fourteen days, a Committee for charity to the beggars met together consisting of several Natives and Europeans and decided that Sub-scriptions to a larger amount as before, should be raised to distribute daily rice to beggars in the morning; hence this kind of distribution began on Friday the 25th ultimo, attended by two European Gentlemen by turns every day, since that time the rumour of this kind of Charity is spreading about, people come from near and far to take advantage of it, so that the number up to this time is already upwards of 3,000, and it is believed, if this kind of Charity continues, the number of those who will take their share will increase.

Padri Elliott of Faizabad

PREACHING IN THE CHAUK, FAIZABAD.

THE taking charge of the work in Faiza-bad marks a turning-point in Mr. Elliott's life. Hitherto, he had not been free to work on his own initiative or have anything like free hand, but had been under the superintendency of older missionaries. Henceforth, he was to be his own superintendent, free to develop the work on the lines that seemed to him most advisable, and to work in those methods most congenial to his temperament. He also took up a burden of responsibility, financial and administrative, that for twenty-two years kept growing heavier and heavier, till exhausted nature could bear no more, and he laid down life and responsibility together. Henceforth, his whole life, with all his thoughts, purposes, prayers, hopes, and anxieties,was to centre round the work in Faizabad, and his name, coupled with that of this Indian city, hitherto unknown in Methodism, was to become a household word-Elliott of Faizabad.

When Mr. Elliott arrived in Faizabad, there was not much work being done, and but a feeble cause. The Hindustani church consisted of two catechists and their families and three other members. There were no out-stations. The only property owned by the Wesleyan Missionary Society was a small chapel in cantonments, somewhat less imposing than a military go-down. It had cost only Rs. 2,000 (£125), and soon became too small for the military congregation. In the Hindustani work, there were two boys' schools and two small girls' schools in the bazaar, with one zanana worker visiting about forty houses. Now we have one of the finest churches in North India, two bungalows for the missionaries, together with a girls' boarding-school in Faizabad, an orphanage at Akbarpur, twelve flourishing village centres -many of them with valuable property and a large staff of evangelists, school teachers, Bible-women, and zanana workers:results that have only been accomplished by much prayer and faith, by careful planning and patient toil.

Mr. Elliott soon saw that if there was to be any great development, his first work must be to obtain satisfactory mission premises. He applied, therefore, to the military authorities for an extension of the site on which the old chapel was built. After many letters, interviews with officials, and much weary waiting, he at length got a splendid piece of land, most conveniently situated both for Hindustani and military work. The officer commanding the station and the cantonment magistrate were both his friends, but he had to thank Lord Roberts, then Commander-in-Chief, for the final sanction.

The first of Mr. Elliott's building operations was performed on the old chapel.

To this he added a fine porch, so out of keeping with it that his brethren jokingly spoke of the old chapel as 'the room behind the porch.' When the new chapel came to be erected, it had to be built in a style of architecture in keeping with the porch, and this was found to cost more than had been anticipated. Like a trueMethodist, he began the work on faith and experienced not a few of the trials of those who walk by faith. At one time, his funds ran out, and he had to dismiss the workpeople on Saturday night, as he had no money for the next week's wages. The following Sunday, during service, a wealthy planter, who was visiting a member of his congregation, noticed his deep depression, and on learning the cause, volunteered to lend him Rs. 4,000-just what he needed to finish the building.

By 1890, the new chapel, mission-house, boarding-school (since much extended), and teacher's house (now the zanana mission-house) were completed, and Mr. Elliott had to face the serious task of clearing off the heavy debts that had accumulated. The debt on the chapel (£600) he wiped off during his first furlough in 1892-3, but at the cost of much overwork and a severe strain on his health. He returned from that furlough worn and tired, but triumphant.

One of Mr. Elliott's greatest achievements was the obtaining permission from the Faizabad municipality to build a pulpit for open-air preaching in the Chauk Bazaar. The story is best told in his own words:

The Chauk, in an Indian city, especially in the afternoons and at nights, presents a unique side of Indian life, and I felt that to get a preaching-place in that great quadrangle of the city of Faizabad was worth almost more to me than even a chapel in the city, because a chapel for some time would be very hard to fill, and then certain classes of natives would, from caste and religious prejudice, never enter it, whereas in the open air, from this iron pulpit, I should be able to catch and draw all classes.

'So I went to the chairman of the Municipal Board and put my case to him thus. I said, "You see, in this city the Hindus have scores of temples and shrines on the thoroughfares, and so also the Muslims have their mosques, but we Christians, who are also a part of the community and pay our share of the taxes, have not a yard of land nor any place of worship to call our own. The request I want to place before you is a very modest one indeed. All I ask for is a circle of land four feet in diameter-nothing more."

Account of Sadhu Sundar Singh

In Annfield, he was taken to the parsonage of the Rev. Y. Dharamjit, who was away on leave. But his servant and adopted son, Bansi were in the house and undertook the responsibility of nursing Sundar Singh.

Later, Dr. Stanley Jones furnished some particulars of Sundar Singh's recovery from the physical effects of the fast. One was recently in Gorakhpur when I had a satisfactory conversation with Dharamjit Singh and his servant. The information that I received from him and his servant seemed very genuine. Dharamjit is an impartial man, with a feeling of responsibility, and on certain points is very clear. This is his story:

"He was on holiday in Basharatpur, near Gorakhpur. His servant wrote from Annfield that Sundar Singh had come in a very weak condition and asked for instruction. Dharamjit told him to take care of him until he returned.

Sundar Singh had been in Kajliban and had fasted. He had then been brought to Rishikesh by some woodcutters who had found him in a thoroughly weakened condition. They handed him over to a non-Christian Sadhu. Later, he came in a cart to Annfield. When Dharamjit returned, he found Sundar Singh still very weak. No entry in a diary was made. There did not seem to be the least doubt that Sundar Singh was not sick but that he was weakened from fasting. No doubt about the whole story ever occurred to Dharamjit because the evidence lay before his eyes.

When Dharamjit returned, Sundar Singh was being fed on milk, and only after eight or ten days was he given any bread. The servant said that when Sundar Singh was brought in, he was so weak that a man had to hold him up. On the first day, he could not speak; only on the second day did he begin to speak. The servant first gave him milk, then soup and sago. He was not sick but only weak from fasting.""

In his little Urdu book about his evangelistic tours (p. 19) Sundar Singh has given a brief account of his spiritual experiences In continuation of this Account is the March of J.R Clifford, father of Ms. PC Clifford. Four young men joined him for this purpose. They were A. S.

Judson, a High School teacher at Unao, J. R. Clifford, an Assistant Tahsildar (subordinate Revenue Official) from Kanpur District, Qudrat Masih from Ambala (who afterwards became a Muslim), and B. Mohan Lal, a Quaker from Bhilsa. All of them were Indians or Anglo-Indians. Bishop Warne of the Methodist Episcopal Church gave them his blessing in Lucknow before they started on their adventurous journey. They left Lucknow on March 31, 1917, the Saturday before Palm Sunday, and proceeded to Dehra Dun. Sundar Singh was attending a conference at Saharanpur, and they waited for him at Dehra Dun to join them; on Wednesday, April 4, they all left on foot for Mussoorie.

J. R. Clifford decided to return home as he found even the hardship of this walk to Mussoorie too much for him. The Rev. W. M. Branch wrote to Sundar Singh not to take Qudrat Masih, and he stayed behind at Mussoorie. Sundar Singh left Mussoorie on Good Friday with the two companions who were left.

Names in the Christian Community

Many Indian Christians have English names like Perfect, Denzil, Robinson, Fredrick, and Newbolt, Ventura, Alexander, Roberts.

Some have kept it in vogue, some were given their surnames by the European Pastors and some are the descendants of the Eurasians.

Most of the times names are kept on the occasion of christening.

Many Christians got commingled with the missionaries and adopted their name.

Some were raised in the Orphanage of the mission and adopted the surname of their Missionaries like in the case of Mr. Prem McCarty.

Some still have the same name as they had before coming into Christ.

There are many other reasons yet to explore.

Politics and Faith

The Chauri Chaura disaster of 1922 not only shook the British Empire in India. The shock waves also affected the Christian Church.

"Hostility towards the British and creased, and that affected the sentiment towards Christian Indians. Christianity was generally seen as a foreign religion", says Savaro Das, who was not a Christian himself at the time of the uprising.

Savaro Das' reaction was obviously typical of the Indians who were converted within the Orebro mission during the freedom struggle. Most of them supported the idea of a free India and probably thought that Gandhi was right. But they distance themselves from the activists and, above all, from their violence. The Christians could not find a third position between violent resistance and passive submission. Most often, all whites were singled out by the freedom movement. They were seen as representatives of colonial power.

The result was that Indians with ties to foreigners branded them as accomplices and agents. Christian Indians were particularly affected by this; Devassin has both religious and political traitors.

Indian nationalism had been linked to Hinduism and anyone who wanted to be both a freedom fighter and Christian had a difficult time.

The missionaries did not speak out against authorities, and especially not against European authorities in a mission country. The mission's work opportunities were considered to depend on it.

But the benefit that the Indian Christians got from the missionaries indirectly showed their inclination towards the British government. My father, being a tahsildar, was slightly biased towards the European government, says PC Clifford. Fellowship pastor Sunder Das, son of Premdas .he is one of the Christians of this time who could not understand the reality of freedom. They lived in the mission, and the missionaries were everything to them.

From Indian Christians within the Orebro mission, there are very few political comments preserved in writing from this time. An exception is a few words from the evangelist Hira Lal in 1923. Very expensive satisfaction that Gandhi's disciples have suffered defeat and count down considerably in a place where they had been very active. "The love of the messiah conquers and defeats everything" is his conclusion. But no one can comment on the unawareness and illiteracy of the people during that time.

Missionary Nils Hansson described what it could be like to become a village and be confused with colonial officials.

"We thought we understood that the people were afraid of us. They probably thought we were in the service of the government. They hated both the white people and the British government.

On asking this question to Dr. LK Das, whose father was the first ordained pastor of Masihi Kalisiya Church Gorakhpur, states that there was no reason for the Indian Christians to hate the British government.

In the 1990s Operation Mobilization leader in Uttar Pradesh, Ganesh Pradhan, states Old people here still have the image of Christianity as a Western religion. The British connection lives in their minds. But the younger generation never experienced colonial power, and slowly this image may be fading.

The Christians in the Örebro mission fields were far from happiness when the British relinquished power in 1947. If many can testify. But that description applies to adults. Among the young people, more and more had begun to study and had gained respect for men like Gandhi and Nehru. Sundar Das was one of them. He went to boarding school in Agra and remembers how the missionary took down Nehru's pictures that the Indian students had put up.

We did not protest openly, but your heart inside. Even though we did not understand what would come with the Indian government, we were unquestioningly in favour of it. The freedom fighters' leaders were our leaders. We wore hand-spun clothes as Gandhi had urged, and we were proud of it. But the Christian dilemma was a difficult one. They wanted political freedom, but they were frightened by the thought of a government hostile to Christianity. If anyone nevertheless tried to join a corner of the freedom movement, it was not easy.

But on the other side, there was a sect that interpreted the missionaries' attitude differently. "The missionaries sided with the British."

Says a descendant of the first Christians in the Örebro mission.

The missionaries resist the mission employees from engaging in politics. The ban applied to other activities that could harm the work of the mission.

The Orebro missionary Frank Rehnstrom wrote afterwards that no thoughtful missionary could fail to sympathize with Indians longing for freedom, their Love of your country, and their desire for a true National existence. But when it came to it, the missionaries apparently failed to give a clear expression to the sympathy.

There was no political inclination of Christians in either of the political parties. Indian National Congress, being the first party after independence, was the only political party to afford support from the Indian Christians; others showed their hostility The missions relied on the support of the British authorities. The British government counted on the loyalty of the missionaries.

Every missionary who applied for permission to enter India had to sign a declaration promising not to do anything that conflicted with the interest of the British government. Commissionary is promised to refrain from political involvement - 'the Missionary pledge' came, however, in practice very often to become identical with loyalty to British Government policy.'

One missionary said that if the Indian National Congress came to power, Christianity and Islam would no longer be tolerated.

On the other hand, PC Clifford notes- "My family and I did not experience any atrocity during the independence."

Eniar Johansson, chairman of the missionary corps, wrote in 1930 that the freedom movement was undoubtedly inspired by the spirit of lawlessness. The English had given evidence of their willingness to hand over control to the Indians. But the rebels did not want peaceful negotiations, but incited the mob, children, and school children to break the law and commit atrocities.

Universities were blocked, trade was paralyzed, laws were trampled on, border people were incited to attack English troops, shops were looted, and forests were cut down,he noted.

Since the British encouraged Christianity, many Christians hoped that colonial rule would endure. When the British sent in troops to crush the freedom struggle, camps were set up to protect mission stations, missionaries, and Indian Christians.

Around independence in 1947, there were terrible acts of violence between Hindus, Muslims, and Sikhs, but hatred was also directed against the British and other whites. Missionary Evert Eriksson was close to becoming one of the many who lost their lives. When he was about to take the train from Gorakhpur to Padrauna, he was warned by Kaleb Massey not to travel. Kaleb Massey took over Evert's ticket and went in his place to give the news to the waiting congregation. The traveler did not return as planned. Four days later, he returned on foot. At the first station, several thousand people had been waiting

for the train to find any European to "sacrifice on Gandhi's altar". They had searched the entire train: Under the armrests, in the toilets, and even in the coal car. But there was no white person.

"If I had been there, I would have had to end my life that day," Evert Eriksson stated afterwards. The views of Christians had varied from time to time, depending on the attitude of the ruling people.

Citation - Excerpts from the book "Det Indiska Undret".

Do the Christian Missionaries Really Convert?

We have done research for more than 2 years on the Christian missionaries. Visiting churches, finding out online records, taking personal interviews, talking to people whose ancestors were in contact with the

Missionaries. From my perspective, Christian missionaries were here to spread their faith. They used to evangelize people by combining it with means like opening mission schools, orphanages, and industrial training centers. They helped the needy, the sick, and those who were helpless. They fed them, educated them, and fulfilled all their primary needs. This is the key reason that the majority of the people of the Christian community are employed in schools, colleges, and hospitals serving people and humanity. We sometimes look at people with prejudice without knowing all the aspects of the situation. We never look at the children who are begging on the roads, who are selling balloons at the traffic signals, and the handicapped who are lying on the pedestrians. These were the people who were served by the missionaries. The Christian missionaries used to nurture them as their own child and tried to shape their career.

The people who start behaving like them, working like them, talking like them, are considered converted. This is the major problem of society. The Christian missionaries did all these good deeds by copying the works that their God did. Christianity is not a religion but a faith that motivates people to follow the path of Christ, by loving each other and helping each other as Jesus did.

Witnesses of CMS

Chand Khan

Hindu by birth, of the Rajput caste, Chand Khan had been early left an orphan by the death of his father (also a soldier) in the war in Afghanistan. The boy wandered about homeless and friendless until Pathan took pity on him and gave him food and shelter. In his house, he was made a Mohammedan.

He afterwards escaped into British territory and enlisted in the regiment to which his father had belonged. Here, while professing to be Mohammedan, he seems to have had no great attachment to that creed. He met with native Christians, whose ways and mode of living pleased him better. While stationed at Allygurh, he became acquainted with a native-Christian catechist, who often came into the neighbourhood for the purpose of preaching the Gospel. This acquaintance ripened into friendship, and the sepoy was much influenced by his new friend's exhortation to cast in his lot with the Christians. The opposition of his The wife, however, held him back. On his regiment moving to Gorruckpore, Chand Khan was desirous of placing his son, a boy of twelve years, in the Mission school. His Mohammedan comrades endeavoured to prevent this, and urged that the boy should be subjected to the initiatory rite of their creed. On the father's refusal, they held a meeting to take steps to induce or coerce him. But the rough, honest soldier was proof against both bribes and threats and, after due instruction, he, his wife, and the boy were baptized. He holds the rank of Naick in his regiment and bears an excellent character. His commanding-officer showed his interest in his conversion by being present at his baptism, just before the departure of the regiment to Bhutan.

We have learned wisdom from the mutiny. There was a time when an officer, instead of countenancing a sepoy under his command in making a public profession of Christianity, would, in every way, have discouraged him and, had he persevered, his case would have been reported to headquarters, and the reply would have been an order for his immediate discharge and remission to his native village. It is well that the lesson has been learned, although at a costly price.

Juala Prasad

Juala Prasad was a merchant from Meerut.

He traveled to Gorakhpur and was suggested to attend the worship at Basharatpur. He attended the church service. His witness is - I have a great revelation to God and hope he will do everything right with my family

The Gatekeeper Hasting John

Last year, it was the day of Good Friday when I went to St. John's Church to attend a program and service before going inside the church. I was sitting at the entrance gate. All of a sudden, I saw a man coming towards the gate. I thought to ask him about Christianity. He described the whole history, and after some time, I asked about his introduction. He told me that he is the gatekeeper of this church, which made me shocked because his dressing and way of talking didn't indicate him to be a gatekeeper. He enunciated that he was a high-caste brahmin Bharadwaj before getting converted. His father was a DRM (Divisional Railway Manager) in the railways, and the British Government sent him to America for research, where he met with an American woman in the same department. He fell in love with her, got married, and came back to India. Mr. Bhardwaj is one of their offspring. Bhardwaj's parental residence is in Lucknow, but he was thrown out of his home because he accepted Christianity. He was treated by the prayers of some catholic priests when he was ill and in a critical condition. He underwent a bible training and was baptized in Peace Tabernacle Church by Ps. Lavin Morar. His wife had already left him, and he now lives alone in a rented room in Basharatpur. Mr. Bhardwaj got his new name "Hasting John' from a Government Officer

Witnesses of the Swedish Mission

Emmanuel:

When I began to study at the evangelist school, our teacher emphasized how important it is for us as witnesses of the Lord to receive the baptism of the Spirit. He often taught us how we could come into possession of the gift of the Spirit. On one occasion, I felt the mighty power of God come over me. If I had not been afraid, I would have received the sealing of the Spirit even then. When the missionaries came down from the mountains in the summer of 1933, and we began a new term at school, we felt that something special was at work. Our teacher told us how Jesus had gone up into the mountains and baptized missionaries in the Holy Spirit. This touched our hearts, and we could not continue with the reading but had to have an opportunity to pour out our hearts in prayer before God. After we had prayed for a few days, I became very sad and opened my heart to the missionary. He understood how I felt. We went in and prayed together. After we prayed for a while, he said to me, 'You will be the first to receive the baptism of the Spirit.' That same afternoon, Jesus sealed me with the Holy Spirit of promise, hallelujah! I also received the gift of speaking in tongues. This is a source of rich blessing to me in spiritual worship. Since the fire fell upon me, my whole life has been changed, and my prayer is that I may be preserved in this anointing and renewed from day to day.

Evangelist Premdash3

When the Spirit of the Lord had been poured out in a very powerful way in Deoria, missionary Rehnström wrote to me and told me how wonderfully God was working among them. In every meeting, someone or a few were baptized in the Holy Spirit. He wrote further: 'I know it will gladden your heart to come here and join in the prayer and rejoice in what is happening here. Ever since you yourself were baptized in the Spirit ten years ago, you have been faithfully praying that Christians may experience salvation in the same way as you. Now come here and praise God with us, and also help us to pray that this work may spread to all our stations. If you have no money, I will pay for the trip. My wife and I traveled to Deoria. I cannot describe what I experienced. Was it really true what I saw? Yes, indeed, there the old evangelist lies on his face before God and confesses that he had resisted the Holy Spirit. What had happened to him? He, who had previously asked whether the Spirit enters the church through the door or the window, lay absorbed in prayer and was seized by the Spirit of God. There, I see several of my fellow workers in the gospel, under the mighty power of God, delivering powerful messages in the Spirit. Some weep over their sins. On others, the Holy Spirit falls. Among these are my wife, her mother, and sister. Yes, many others with them have the same blessed experience. Oh, what meetings! The Holy Spirit was powerfully poured out upon us. I wept for joy and rejoiced over what I saw and heard. I never thought that something so wonderful would happen among us.

During these days that I was among God's people in Deoria, I was renewed in my spirit. Hallelujah!These were unforgettable days before the Lord, when many rededicated their lives to the Lord. The Spirit fell upon these, and their lives were greatly changed. But some did not want to open their hearts to God, and therefore they did not get to taste the powers of the world to come. For them, these glad tidings were of no use. If everyone in our mission had received the blessing, it would have been wonderful.

Hira Firangi:

I was born of believing parents and have been in the mission since I was a little boy. While working in the carpentry shop in Deoria, I came to a living faith in Christ and received God's call to be an evangelist, which is why I had to start in the evangelist school. The necessity of being filled with the Holy Spirit in the same way as the apostles was often emphasized. Surely I longed to be a part made by the fullness of the Spirit. There was no real need, however, until the missionaries Rehnströms returned from the mountains in the summer of 1933, where they had a new encounter with God. We were very moved when we heard their stories of how God had worked up in the mountains and baptized several missionaries in the Holy Spirit. We felt that a new power rested over our meetings. When the Holy Spirit shed His light on my life, much hidden sin was revealed, which was abominable before God. In this way, my heart was prepared for the Holy Spirit. Through confession of sin, both before God and men, and prayer for forgiveness, the burdens were lifted, and peace filled my heart.

After praying for a few days, Emanuel, my classmate in the evangelistic school, was baptized in the Holy Spirit and spoke in tongues. When the rest of us saw how his face shone with joy as he spoke in a foreign tongue, we were all touched beyond measure and began to pray as never before. A few days later, when I heard at a meeting how necessary it is to open one's whole heart and seek God, since He pours out His Spirit so abundantly upon us, the need became so great that I could not leave the prayer corner until the Holy Spirit had fallen upon me. Oh, how wonderful! My whole life was changed. Today, I thank God that I was able to experience something so wonderful. It is a year and a half since I was baptized in the Spirit and received the gift of speaking in tongues. The same fire burns in my heart today.

Pastor Acheson

The Directory of CMS Gorakhpur

Headquarters of the District. A moist and rainy place. The commerce is chiefly confined to the export of agricultural produce.

Population, 51,117; Protestant Indian Christians, 870. Mission in the field. The Church Missionary Society. Resident Missionaries, 4.

Churches, 2; Communicants, 387. Pastor-The Rev. John Qalander.

1. Christ Church-Was built by H. E. I. Company in 1827, and consecrated in 1841. Almost all the Christian children born in the District have been baptized in this Church.
2. St. Andrew's Church-On August 30, 1897, the foundation stone was laid.

Sunday Schools, 2; Scholars, 222.

Mission Schools, 13; 2 High Schools, 2 Middle Schools, 5 Primary Schools, 3 Christian Schools. 893 students; 323 Indian Christian students.

C. M. S. HIGH SCHOOL.

Head Master.-S. K. D. Gupta, Esq., B.A. ALINAGAR SCHOOL, C. M. S,

Head Master.-Mr. Chatterji. Swinton School, C. M. S. Headmaster, Mr. Masih Dayal.

President Mrs. F. Ellwood (Y. W.C. A).

INDIAN CHRISTIAN ASSOCIATION.

President- D. Thomas, Esq., B.A.

Vice-President- S. K. D. Gupta, Esq., B.A.

Secretary- George M. D. Singh, Esq. Aiyub, J.

Members. Basano. Clive, J. Das, V. Dass, Miss. Dayal, J.M., Mrs. Dharmjit, C. K. Edward, Gangoli, Mrs. Heney, P. Japhat, Kenoz, A. Lacy, C. J. Lacy, Prabhu Das. Lal, Joshua, Morris, M. Mukerji, M. M. Mukerji, M., Mrs. Nundy, A. Nundy, Mrs. Raphael, A. Roy, Ronghai. Rufus, J. A. Seni, E. J. Shem, J. H. Singh, E. M. D., Mrs. Stephen, J. Thomas, H.

Indian Christian Mission Agents. Rev. John Qalander-Pastor.

Mr. S. K. D. Gupta, B.A., Head Master, C. M. S. High School. Mr. Chatterji, Head Master, Alinagar High School.

Masih Dayal, Head Master, Swinton School.

L. Masih Dayal, Head Master, Girls' School.

Miss Dass, Headmistress, Girls' School. Vincent, Teacher, Girls' School.

Mary Dharmjit, Head Teacher, Girls' School, Mrs. Hannah, Matron, Girls' Orphanage.

Mr. Joshua Lal, House Father, Boys' Orphanage.

A. L. Lacy, Foreman, C. M. S. Press.

G. Masih Dayal, Catechist, C. M. S.

S. Mitthoo

Durga Charan Dey Gabriel Ventura

B. Cornelius Johoshaphat Dharmjit, James Jackson

P. Obadiah, Reader Nathaniel

H. Garudin, Preacher, Indian Christian Lawyers.

A. Nundy, Esq., Bar.-at-Law.

D. Thomas, Esq., B.A., High Court Vakil.

An Indian Christian who has visited foreign countries.

A. Nundy, Esq., Bar.-at-Law

Subscriptions made to the Gorruckpore Mission

R.H Clifford Esq. Ahmad Ali Shah sahib Lt. T. Montriou B Alone, Esq. Mrs. White Col Lamb, Lt. Gubbins, Major Bruce, Dr. Cheke, Lt. Bransford C. Brooke, Esq. Lt. Branson J.H Bridgman, Esq. Baboo K Dan Singh

The Paidleyganj Cemetery

The Paidleyganj Cemetery is about 200 years old and was particularly meant for the Europeans. Some of the famous graves include The Indigo Planter, Campiers of

Campierganj Peppe's of Birdpur Hugh Gibbon of Birdpur Mr. Sym of Glasgow, Jungle Padrauna Grantee Thomas Edwin, son of Michael Wilkinson, the missionary.

Lt. John Harriet Gerrard Son of S Knowles, missionary to Gonda. Lt. Teed drowned at the Domingarh lake Daughter of Lt. T Monstriou Daughter of Joshua Carter, collector of Gorruckpore Reade Family Carl Hammarsten, Swedish Missionary, Antoine Coutiere, Barhalgunj Mr. Coomb, Indigo Planter, Major Henry Hamilton Child of Mr. JJ Holdsworth of Lehra estate. Charles Vipan Esq, forest conservator, Bengalis - Kundu, Ganguli, and Dass

Sources

©Take this child by Mary Warburton Booth
©Det Indiska Undret by Arne Bengtsson
Shaharnama Gorakhpur by Dr Ved Prakash Pandey
© H.R Nevill Gazetteer 1909 The Indian Boken
Etv Bharat News Article
The Hindustan Times
Unacademy Chauri Chaura Incident
A.G Pentecostal Archives
Amar Ujala Article Trailblazers of God
GRD official webpage

Glimpses of Christian India by Ms. Ellwood Commoners
Struggles in Life by Dr. SNM Tripathi
Leaves from a policeman's diary By B.N Lahiri
Padri Elliott of Faizabad
14th Annual Report of the Ghazeepore mission Anglo Indian by Dr. Lal Bahadur Verma
Annual Report Orebro Mission
Writings compiled by A.R Cavalier
The Indian Mutiny by Charles Wingfield
© The Gospel in Gonda by S. Knowles
Directory of Protestant Indian Christians
By Modak. S

Credits -

I would like to express my gratitude to

Ravindra Bhalerao
Awani McCarty
Dr. LK Das
Cyrill family
Lazarus family
Potter family
Abhishikt Roberts

They were always available to help us out in providing information and assistance whenever it was needed.